"This workbook provides teens with a step-by-step guide for dealing with their worries and increasing helpful behaviors. Teens will be able to relate to the examples and learn concrete strategies to manage anxiety related to school, procrastination, friendships, and social media. 'Junk mail thoughts' is a particularly interesting way to help teens understand the concept of anxious self-talk and manage worry. This excellent new resource is highly recommended for both teens and the professionals who work with them."

—**Laura C. Reigada, PhD**, associate professor of psychology at the City University of New York at Brooklyn College and The Graduate Center

"Jamie Micco has crafted a clear, informative, and easy-to-read resource that will be useful for any teen struggling with anxiety, as well as their loved ones. The text details empirically supported treatment components to help fight anxiety in a practical, step-by-step manner. Micco should be congratulated for this masterful work, which fills a critical gap in the field for this age-group."

—**Eric Storch, PhD**, All Children's Hospital Guild; endowed chair and professor at the University of South Florida

"This is an excellent resource for anxious teens, and for the clinicians who work with them. The workbook reviews key cognitive behavioral therapy (CBT) strategies and skills, is easy to follow, and includes helpful and relatable examples. The exercises for each section are brief and right on point. As an added bonus, Jamie Micco has included online exercises to complement the written text. I absolutely plan to recommend this book to my clients."

—**Kathryn D. Boger, PhD, ABPP**, board-certified clinical child and adolescent psychologist specializing in CBT, and director of the McLean Hospital Anxiety Mastery Program

"With creativity, clarity, and fun, Jamie Micco offers teens effective cognitive behavioral strategies to deal with the 'junk mail thoughts' and unhelpful behaviors that come along with chronic worry. Whether teens are dealing with mild or severe chronic worry, they will greatly benefit from reading this book and completing all exercises. This is a must-read for teens!"

> —**Patricia E. Zurita Ona, PsyD**, psychologist at the East Bay Behavior Therapy Center, and coauthor of *Mind and Emotions*

the worry workbook for teens

effective cbt strategies to break the cycle of chronic worry & anxiety

JAMIE A. MICCO, PhD

Instant Help Books
An Imprint of New Harbinger Publications, Inc.

Publisher's Note

Distributed in Canada by Raincoast Books

Copyright © 2017 by Jamie A. Micco
        Instant Help Books
        An imprint of New Harbinger Publications, Inc.
        5674 Shattuck Avenue
        Oakland, CA 94609
        www.newharbinger.com

Cover design by Amy Shoup

Acquired by Tesilya Hanauer

Edited by Jean Blomquist

Library of Congress Cataloging-in-Publication Data

Names: Micco, Jamie A., author.
Title: The worry workbook for teens : effective CBT strategies to break the cycle of chronic worry and anxiety / Jamie A. Micco, PhD.
Description: Oakland, CA : New Harbinger Publications, Inc., [2017] | Includes bibliographical references.
Identifiers: LCCN 2016057902 (print) | LCCN 2017004048 (ebook) | ISBN 9781626255845 (paperback) | ISBN 9781626255852 (pdf e-book) | ISBN 9781626255869 (epub) | ISBN 9781626255852 (PDF e-book) | ISBN 9781626255869 (ePub)
Subjects: LCSH: Anxiety in adolescence--Treatment. | Worry in adolescence--Treatment. | Cognitive therapy.
Classification: LCC RJ506.A58 M53 2017 (print) | LCC RJ506.A58 (ebook) | DDC 616.85/2200835--dc23
LC record available at https://lccn.loc.gov/2016057902

19   18   17

10   9   8   7   6   5   4   3   2   1   First Printing

Contents

Section Four: Changing Unhelpful Behavior

Section Five: Mind-Body Strategies to Reduce Worry

Section Six: Conclusion

introduction: a letter to the reader

Welcome to *The Worry Workbook for Teens: Effective CBT Strategies to Break the Cycle of Chronic Worry and Anxiety*! Cognitive behavioral therapy (CBT) is a hands-on program that helps people to develop the skills they need to cope with anxiety and change their behavior to reduce the intensity and frequency of their worries. This workbook presents CBT strategies intended to break down the cycle of thoughts, emotions, physical feelings, and behaviors that worried teens tend to experience.

Although you can dive into the workbook activities in whatever order you choose, you'll find that the workbook is organized by type of activity. The first section helps you understand the difference between typical "everyday" types of worry and chronic, difficult-to-control worry that gets in the way of living your life. The second section goes further into the types of unhelpful thoughts that increase your anxiety—I call these "junk mail thinking." The third section helps you develop skills for dealing with your junk mail thoughts.

The fourth section of the workbook focuses on changes you can make in your behavior that will further challenge your anxious thoughts. It provides step-by-step instructions for getting rid of behaviors that take time away from activities you'd rather be doing. This section also offers strategies to address common sources of worry, including the excessive use of social media.

In the fifth section, you'll learn mind-body techniques—such as how to relax your body—that make you less vulnerable to the stress that fuels worry and anxiety. The workbook concludes with how to maintain the improvements you've made by practicing the CBT strategies presented here.

As a bonus to this workbook, you can access additional activities and exercises online. In these activities, you'll learn to identify exactly what you're worried about and to challenge the common belief that worry is protective. You'll also learn about managing your schedule and reducing anxiety about taking tests. The online exercises will deepen the skills that you build in this workbook. Please visit http://www .newharbinger.com/35845 to download these bonus activities and exercises.

Many teens will find it sufficient to work through the exercises independently or with the support of their parents. However, others will benefit from using the strategies offered here in their work with a qualified mental health professional such as

- a therapist who specializes in CBT for youth with anxiety disorders—this may be a licensed clinical or counseling psychologist (PhD or PsyD), social worker (LICSW), psychiatrist (MD), or licensed mental health counselor (LMHC);

- a medical doctor (psychiatrist or primary care doctor), who can determine if medication would further help you manage your anxiety; or

- a guidance counselor or school psychologist, who can help you apply these strategies to situations that come up at school or with peers.

If you think you might need additional help or support from one or more of these professionals, talk with your parents, school counselor, or primary care doctor (or pediatrician)—they can make a plan to ensure you're getting the help you need.

Congratulations as you get started with this workbook. You're taking the first steps toward breaking your own personal worry cycle!

Section One

Understanding Worry

1   what is worry, and when is it a problem?

for you to know

Everybody worries sometimes. *Worry* is a thought process that focuses on what will happen in the future; it often involves thinking of all the ways a situation could turn out (especially the ways it could turn out badly). To some extent, worry helps us prepare and come up with solutions for all the problems that could arise. As such, people tend to worry when there's good reason to do so. For example, if you've been getting low grades on many of your recent math tests, you might worry about an exam you have tomorrow; if your grandfather is in the hospital, you might worry about his future health.

On the other hand, some people worry *excessively*—they worry frequently about many different aspects of their life, above and beyond what would be considered typical or helpful. Oftentimes, these worries are about situations that are unlikely to happen or about situations the person has no control over. On other occasions, worriers may think in excruciating detail about events in the far future that may be controllable, but there's little use in thinking about them now. These worries tend to take up a lot of time and energy.

Consider Amanda, a fifteen-year-old high school sophomore. She earns good grades in honors classes, plays on the varsity soccer team, and has several close friends. She gets along well with her parents and her younger sister. However, Amanda spends many hours a day worrying about how she might mess up and lose everything she has worked hard for. She worries about getting poor grades, letting down her soccer team and losing her varsity position, and upsetting or offending her friends. As a result, she spends more time studying than she needs to, constantly checks in with her soccer coach to make sure he thinks she's doing what she's supposed to, and often asks her friends if they're mad at her. Amanda complains of feeling "so tired" most of the time, and she has stomachaches that affect her appetite.

Like Amanda, some people with intense, frequent worry that interferes with their lives meet criteria for *generalized anxiety disorder* (GAD). GAD in teenagers is characterized by (1) frequent (that is, more days than not), excessive, and difficult-to-control worry about two or more areas of life (for example, school, friendships, health, safety); (2) one or more physical or cognitive symptoms, such as restlessness, headaches, difficulty sleeping, grouchiness, and poor concentration; and (3) a duration of at least six months (American Psychiatric Association 2013). The worries and physical/cognitive symptoms also get in the way of life somehow—for example, difficulty going to school or completing schoolwork, or not having enough time to spend with friends because the worries are so time consuming.

About 3 percent of American teenagers (ages thirteen to eighteen) have GAD, though many more teens have unhelpful worry that falls short of meeting criteria for GAD (Burstein et al. 2014)—for example, those who are prone to worry or stress, but the worries do not yet interfere with school performance or social relationships. This workbook is intended for teenagers who are bothered by worries and want to learn helpful anxiety management strategies, whether or not they have a diagnosis of GAD.

for you to do

Are worries a problem for you? After reading each statement below, circle whether you agree or disagree that the statement describes you:

I worry about a lot of different things in my life.	Agree	Disagree
People tell me I worry more than I need to.	Agree	Disagree
I'm worried about something most days.	Agree	Disagree
It's hard for me to stop my worries.	Agree	Disagree
I've been a worrier for at least six months.	Agree	Disagree
My worries take up an hour or more of my day.	Agree	Disagree
My worries make me do things I don't really need to do, like ask for reassurance from my family and friends, study more than I need to, look up information about my worries online, and so on.	Agree	Disagree
When I'm worried, I feel physically uncomfortable (that is, I get stomachaches or headaches, have trouble sleeping or low energy, or have trouble concentrating).	Agree	Disagree

Count the number of times you circled "Agree."

If zero, then worry is unlikely to be a significant problem for you.

If one to four, worry may be causing you problems that can be worked on using strategies from this book.

If five or more, your worry is likely problematic. This workbook will help you develop strategies to manage your worry, but you may benefit from additional help from a school counselor, therapist, or psychiatrist.

more to do

Consider how worry interferes in your life. The checklist below will help you figure out the extent to which worry takes up your time and energy or gets in your way.

Worry causes me to…

☐ procrastinate or have trouble getting my schoolwork done on time.

☐ spend more time than I need to on my schoolwork.

☐ avoid certain situations at school (for example, giving class presentations, going to the cafeteria, or asking for help).

☐ avoid going to school altogether.

☐ ask my teachers a lot of questions or for more help than I really need.

☐ frequently visit the nurse or school counselor.

☐ feel panicky or "blank out" when I'm taking a test or quiz.

☐ avoid trying out for sports, theater, music, or other activities.

☐ overprepare or overpractice for my extracurricular activities.

☐ do more than I really need to make sure people like me or don't get mad at me.

☐ ask my friends a lot if everything is okay or if they're mad at me.

☐ check over my text messages for signs that my friends are upset with me.

☐ avoid social situations (for example, parties, hanging out with friends, or going to the mall).

☐ check my appearance a lot or spend more time than most teens getting ready in the morning.

☐ frequently check the Internet for information on things I'm worried about.

☐ have difficulty making decisions.

☐ ask my parents or other family members for a lot of reassurance or to look for evidence they think that I'm doing things the "right" way.

☐ ask my family members to solve my problems for me.

☐ snap at my family members because I'm feeling so irritable.

☐ have frequent trouble falling or staying sleeping.

☐ (other) _____

☐ (other) _____

☐ (other) _____

Keep in mind the areas of interference you've checked off above—this will help you focus your efforts as you work through the strategies presented in this workbook. These strategies will certainly take hard work and consistent practice, but you can do it! With persistence, your worries will become less intense, more manageable, and much less of an obstacle to doing what's important to you in life.

for you to know

Has anyone ever said to you, "Don't worry" or "Just calm down"? If only it were that simple! It takes time and practice to learn strategies that will reduce your worry, but the first step is straightforward: break down your worry into more manageable parts. Different aspects of worry play off of one another to make you feel more and more anxious, a process called the "worry cycle." Components of the worry cycle include these:

- **Trigger:** This starts the worry cycle. It's often a particular event or situation (for example, an argument with your parents, a big test at school, a friend who isn't returning your message, and so on), but sometimes a thought or a feeling triggers the worry cycle, even if nothing stressful is happening.

- **Emotions:** Often you notice emotions first: you might feel anxious, frustrated, scared, angry, disappointed, or other emotions.

- **Physical feelings:** If you pay close attention, your body may signal to you that it's stressed: your neck and shoulder muscles tighten, your heart beats faster, you can't catch your breath, or your head aches. Some teens report having panic attacks, when four or more intense physical symptoms happen at once (for example, heart racing, light-headedness, shortness of breath, tingling in hands and feet, sudden hot or cold feelings). A panic attack isn't dangerous and usually passes within a few minutes, if you just let it run its course.

- **Thoughts:** These pop into your head in response to the trigger, often in the form of "what if?" questions. For instance, *What if I fail my test?* or *What if I get a terrible disease?*

- **Behaviors:** These are actions you take in response to your anxious feelings and thoughts. Sometimes, though, a "behavior" is to *avoid* doing something—for example, you might choose to stay home from school to avoid a test you think you'll fail, or you might avoid trying out for soccer for fear the coaches will think you're not good enough for the team.

Worry cycle components can intensify one another to make your anxiety worse. Consider Ashley, a fourteen-year-old girl who worries a lot about her family's health and safety. She gets invited to spend the night at her friend's house, but she knows that her parents are going out that night and she worries they won't come home safely. See how this plays out in her worry cycle:

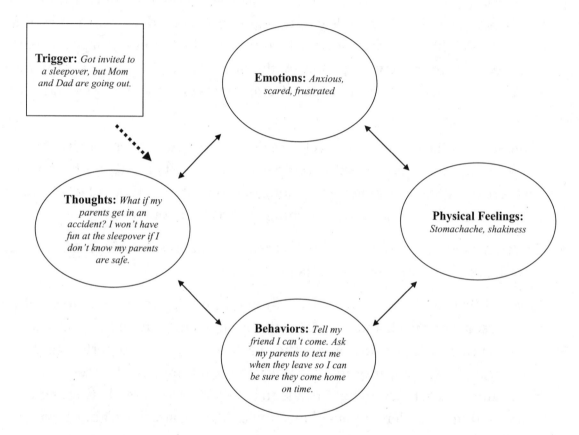

Notice the arrows between the parts of Ashley's worry cycle—they show how each part of the cycle can amplify the next. Ashley's thought that something bad might happen to her parents increases her worry and her physical feelings of anxiety; these feelings in turn intensify her worry thoughts. Her physical and emotional discomfort leads to her decision to stay home and check up on her parents. This may decrease her discomfort temporarily, but over time, her avoidance feeds into her belief that she has to keep track of her parents in order for them to stay safe. Though this thought is probably not true, she avoids all situations that would allow her to test it out. So, in future situations like this, Ashley will probably be just as worried.

for you to do

Think of a recent time when you felt very worried. Following Ashley's example, map out your trigger, emotions, thoughts, physical feelings, and behaviors using the chart below.

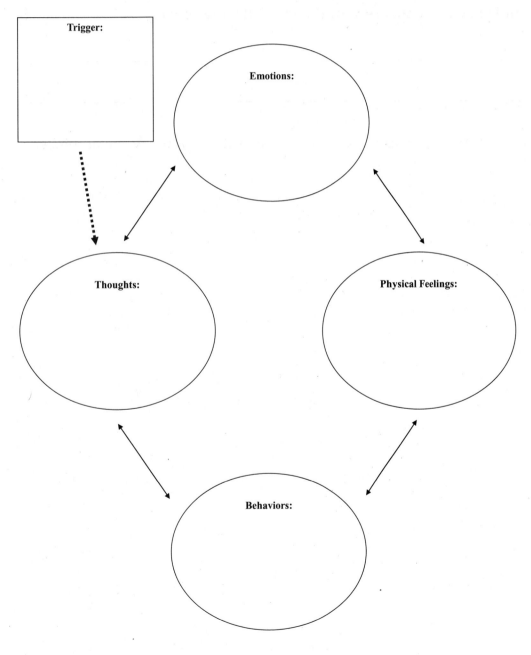

Did your thoughts influence your emotions or physical feelings? If so, describe:

_____

_____

Did your behaviors influence your thoughts? If so, describe:

_____

_____

To download another helpful exercise, please visit http://www.newharbinger.com
/35845.

Section Two

Junk Mail Thinking

3 junk mail thoughts

for you to know

We're bombarded with all sorts of thoughts throughout the day. Some thoughts are really important (that formula for math class you need to remember for a test), and other thoughts are fairly trivial (*Should I eat an apple or chips for a snack?*). Worry thoughts *feel* important, but actually have many flaws if you look carefully. Imagine you have a thought "filter" that selects the important or meaningful thoughts and screens out those that are unhelpful or don't make sense. For people who worry a lot, it's as if that thought filter is broken—it lets in all sorts of thoughts that would have been better to ignore. Another way to think about this is that the worry thoughts are like junk mail—they're better thrown away than read. *Junk mail thoughts* are distortions that keep you from being able to see the big picture.

Eliza is at lunch with her friends at school. Everyone is talking about exams and plans for the weekend. One of her friends mentions how easy the geometry final was for her. Eliza thinks, *I thought that test was hard. Maybe I'm really bad at studying—or maybe I'm terrible at math. How am I going to get into college if I don't do well in math?* Meanwhile, another friend starts talking about her plans to go to a concert with a few other girls this weekend. Eliza starts to wonder why she wasn't invited: *Are my friends sick of me? I hardly ever go to concerts. My friends do much more exciting things than I do.*

Eliza gets so caught up with her thoughts that it's hard for her to participate in the conversation. Her interpretations of her friends' comments cause her to feel anxious, and she loses her appetite. Her worries are so intense, that it's hard for her to remember that she has always gotten As and Bs in math, and that college applications focus on a lot more than math grades anyway. She also isn't focusing on the fact that her friends often ask her to hang out, and that she even went to a concert a month ago. Rather, she's stuck on the junk mail thoughts, which distract her, increase her anxiety, and keep her from looking at the big picture.

for you to do

For each scenario below, circle the junk mail thoughts (that is, unhelpful, distorted thoughts) and underline thoughts you think would be more helpful or accurate.

It's the day of your big soccer tournament. You're the goalie, and you've been working hard all season, but certain shots are still tough for you to block. The opposing team has a reputation for scoring a lot of goals.

- *It's going to be so embarrassing when I can't block the shots. I just know I'm going to choke.*

- *I've got a great team backing me up, and I've gotten much better at blocking shots this season.*

- *Even if I let some shots through, that doesn't mean I won't block others. Besides, our team can score goals, too.*

- *Coach will be so mad when I mess up. He'll kick me off the varsity team, and that will look bad on my college applications.*

Your parents went out to dinner with friends and left you at home to watch your younger sister. They said they'd be home around 9:30 p.m., but it is 9:45 and they're not back yet.

- *They're probably having a good time and decided to stay later.*

- *What if they got into a car accident?*

- *The restaurant is pretty far away—it's not that late, anyway.*

- *If they don't come home, I have no idea what I'll do!*

You have an English essay due in two days on a book that was difficult to understand. You've written only a paragraph so far.

- *I'm never going to get this done.*

- *The teacher will think I'm an idiot.*

- *I still have two days—I can do three paragraphs today and three tomorrow.*

- *I'll write about the parts of the book that I do understand—it's okay if I don't put everything in the essay.*

more to do

For the next few days, keep a list of thoughts that pop into your head when you feel worried or are confronted with a stressful trigger (that is, a situation, thought, or feeling that makes you feel anxious). Be as specific and detailed as possible when writing down your thoughts. (For guidance on how to do this, see Activity 27, What Exactly Am I Worried About? at http://www.newharbinger.com/35845.) Rate how worried each thought makes you feel on a scale from 0 (not at all) to 10 (very much). Also rate how much the thought helps you in the situation, using the 0 to 10 scale. Finally, determine if the thought is junk mail and write yes/no/maybe. Note: If the thought creates high levels of worry and has low levels of helpfulness, it is likely junk mail. See the first line on the chart as an example from Eliza's situation.

Since it's unlikely that you'll be carrying this book around at all times, consider jotting your worry thoughts down on a piece of paper or in your phone, and then return to this page to complete the chart. Also consider copying this chart or downloading it from our website (http://www.newharbinger.com/35845) and printing it out to carry with you. Then refer to the chart as you do the other activities that focus on junk mail thinking.

Date	Trigger	Thought	Worry level (0–10)	Helpfulness (0–10)	Junk mail thought? Yes/No/Maybe
Example: 10/13	Friends are talking about their weekend plans.	Are my friends sick of me? I hardly ever go to concerts. My friends do much more exciting things than I do.	8	3	Yes

all-or-nothing thinking 4

for you to know

All-or-nothing thinking is a type of distorted thinking (or "junk mail") that your worry sends you, and is common among perfectionists. *All-or-nothing thinking* (also known as "black-and-white thinking") involves evaluating or judging a situation using extreme categories and not noticing that there may be a more balanced explanation for what's going on. All-or-nothing thoughts may include words like "always" or "never" instead of more nuanced words like "sometimes" or "usually." For example, someone who worries a lot about grades might be upset when she gets a B on an essay because she believes that only As are "acceptable," and anything less is "always a failure." Another person might worry about being liked by his peers. He thinks that he must always be "super funny, smart, and good at sports or music" in order to be well liked. Both imagine bad things happening if they fall short of their very high standards, and they have trouble recognizing that a B is still a good grade, or that people still want to be friends with someone who isn't perfect at everything.

Matt is a seventeen-year-old junior in high school who has a lot of activities on his plate. He's taking several honors classes, preparing for the SAT, and running track. Lately, he's been putting off his homework until it piles up. When he contemplates starting his homework, he thinks, *This has to be perfect* or *If I don't have enough time to get it all done, there's no point in doing anything.* He then makes a deal with himself that he can put off the work because *This weekend, I'll get it all done.* By the weekend, though, he feels so overwhelmed by the catch-up work he has to do that he continues to avoid it. He's also discouraged with his SAT preparation because he thinks his scores should improve a lot each time he takes another practice test. He thinks, *I must be doing something wrong because my score was only twenty points higher than last time.* Matt's all-or-nothing thinking leads him to impossibly high standards—standards that he can't always meet. This is so discouraging that he can't effectively do his work. Imagine how different he would feel if he could tell himself, *It's okay if my work isn't perfect. I'll just do the best I can to get it done.*

for you to do

For each scenario below, circle examples of all-or-nothing thinking. Next, place a star by thoughts that represent a more balanced interpretation of what's happening—in other words, a thought that takes all information into consideration.

Your parents tell you there's a family reunion this weekend and everyone in your family has to go.

* *I hate family reunions. I always have a terrible time.*

* *It might rain that day, and then the reunion will be ruined.*

* *Even though some parts of the reunion are boring, I usually like the food and seeing my cousin Jon.*

Your coach encourages you to try out for an elite gymnastics team.

* *Whether or not I make the team, it would be good experience to try out and get some feedback on how to improve.*

* *I'll never make the team. You have to be amazing to make it, and I'm terrible.*

* *Although my floor routine could use some work, I've been getting good scores on my other skills.*

You're starting at a new school and attend an orientation where you meet some classmates.

* *I can tell right away if someone's going to be my friend. The others aren't worth getting to know.*

* *I'll introduce myself to as many people as I can. I'm bound to find people with whom I share at least a few things in common.*

* *I'm sure I'll only like the other athletes.*

more to do

This exercise will help you identify your own all-or-nothing thinking while considering more balanced alternative thoughts. You can practice this skill whenever all-or-nothing thinking shows up. (For additional guidance on challenging your thoughts, see Activity 11.)

This week, pay attention to times when you have all-or-nothing thoughts. Remember, these thoughts are most likely to come up when you're evaluating yourself or others (for example, parents, friends, teachers, and so on). Record two instances of all-or-nothing thinking below, and counter those thoughts by generating a more balanced interpretation, using this example as a guide:

Situation: *My parents said I can't stay over my friend's house Friday night because we have too much going on the next day.*

All-or-nothing thought(s): *My parents never let me do anything I want to do. My friend won't invite me over again.*

More balanced thoughts: *There are times my parents let me do things—last week I got to go to the football game with friends. My friend will probably understand if I suggest another time for us to hang out.*

Now it's your turn:

Situation: _____

All-or-nothing thought(s): _____

_____

_____

_____

What would be a more balanced thought? _____

_____

_____

Situation: _____

All-or-nothing thought(s): _____

_____

_____

_____

What would be a more balanced thought? _____

_____

_____

catastrophizing 5

for you to know

You may be familiar with the word "catastrophe." A *catastrophe* is a disaster, like a devastating hurricane that destroys homes, or a big business that goes bankrupt and causes people to lose their jobs. *Catastrophizing* (also known as "catastrophic thinking") is a type of distorted thought that makes it seem like a situation is going to be a disaster when that's really unlikely. When you catastrophize, you tend to believe that the situation will be so awful that you won't be able to handle it or cope with your feelings about it.

Basically, when you catastrophize, you imagine that your worst fears will come true. The resulting anxiety feels so overwhelming that it's hard to consider evidence that what you fear is actually unlikely. Here are a few examples of catastrophizing: (1) seeing a rash on your arm, looking up your symptoms on the Internet, and concluding that you have a deadly illness; (2) overhearing your parents arguing and thinking that means they're going to divorce; and (3) being on an airplane that's experiencing some turbulence and believing that means the plane will crash.

Liz is a fourteen-year-old girl who's in the ninth grade at a large school. Her history teacher asks the class to write about their opinion on a current event and then to give a five-minute oral presentation to the class summarizing what they wrote. Liz hates oral presentations. As she prepares, she imagines that the worst will happen. She thinks, *I'm going to forget everything and stand there without anything to say.* Then, *What if I get so anxious that I throw up? Everyone will think there's something really wrong with me, or they'll just start laughing.* She imagines the class pointing and laughing at her as she runs out of the room, too embarrassed to ever return. She gets so caught up in her catastrophic thinking that she doesn't consider that she could end up doing just fine on her presentation and that it's pretty unlikely that she'd throw up.

for you to do

This exercise will help you get in the habit of identifying and countering your tendency to catastrophize. For each situation, challenge the catastrophic thought by coming up with a less disastrous way the situation could turn out, using this example as a guide.

Situation: Your parents take an airplane across the country.

Catastrophic thought: *That's such a long way to go—their plane is going to crash!*

What is another, more positive way the situation could turn out?

Nothing will happen—the plane will take off and land without trouble.

Situation: At your friend's birthday party, you bump into the most popular girl in your class and spill your drink on her.

Catastrophic thought: *She's going to tell everyone, and they'll all hate me!*

What is another, more positive way the situation could turn out?

_____

_____

Situation: You're learning to drive. You back into a mailbox and put a small dent in the back bumper.

Catastrophic thought: *My parents will never let me drive the car again. It'll be years before I can get my license.*

What is another, more positive way the situation could turn out?

_____

_____

Situation: It's your first night at a two-week summer program. You feel anxious. Your heart is racing and you don't have much of an appetite.

Catastrophic thought: *I'm going to panic and it will last the whole two weeks!*

What is another, more positive way the situation could turn out?

_____

_____

more to do

Tackle your own catastrophic thinking. Consider recent situations when you worried that the worst would happen. Pick two of those situations to complete this exercise.

Situation: _____

Catastrophic thoughts: _____

_____

Think of one or two more positive ways the situation could turn out:

_____

_____

_____

What is most likely to happen and why?

_____

_____

_____

_____

Situation: _____

Catastrophic thoughts: _____

_____

Think of one or two more positive ways the situation could turn out:

_____

_____

_____

What is most likely to happen and why?

_____

_____

_____

_____

6 mind reading

for you to know

Are you concerned about making a good impression, being well liked, and not upsetting anyone? If so, you may believe you're not doing a good enough job making others happy, which leads to thoughts that other people are judging you negatively. For example, imagine passing a friend in the hall at school and saying hi. The friend keeps looking ahead and doesn't acknowledge you. You think, *What did I do wrong? Is he mad at me? Maybe he doesn't want to be friends anymore.* Or, you have to ask the boss at your after-school job for time off. As you walk into the boss's office, you think, *She's going to be mad at me. She'll think I'm not a reliable worker.* In both situations, you assume the most negative explanation is true. This type of junk mail thought—believing others are negatively evaluating you—is called *mind reading.*

Unless you have developed special powers, it's unlikely you can say with total certainty what another person is thinking. This uncertainty can increase your anxiety and cause you to try to gain certainty through repeated questioning ("Are you mad at me?") or scanning people's faces for signs of what they're thinking. However, these behaviors tend to make you feel *more* anxious over time. The goal is to accept that you don't know for sure what others are thinking; this means that a more positive interpretation is as likely (if not more likely) than a negative interpretation. Remember the friend who passed you in the hall and didn't say hi? He may have been thinking about everything he had to do that day and just didn't see you. Your boss? She may be used to schedule fluctuations, so it's no big deal to give you some time off.

Caleb and two of his friends have been talking about hanging out on Friday night but haven't made specific plans yet. It's Thursday evening, so Caleb texts his friends and suggests going to the football game and then grabbing pizza. One of his friends texts back with just "K," and two hours later his other friend still hasn't replied. Caleb starts to feel anxious. He imagines that his friends think his idea is boring and then thinks of every time he may have offended or annoyed his friends in the past few weeks. He thinks, *Maybe they're mad at me or just sick of me. They probably don't want to hang out at all*. Caleb asks his older brother what he thinks is going on, and his brother encourages him to remember the many times these same friends have asked Caleb to hang out recently. He asks Caleb if there might be another explanation for their lack of response. After some thought, Caleb remembers that both of his friends have basketball practice on Thursdays and a big chemistry test the next day; he thinks it's possible his friends just don't have time to plan for tomorrow right now.

for you to do

To identify and challenge mind reading, try this exercise over the next few weeks. Do it whenever you're worried someone might be displeased with you or criticizing you. See the example below as a guide:

Situation: I was sick last week and have to ask my teacher for an extension on my essay.

Mind-reading thought: *He'll think I should have planned further ahead or else worked all weekend to get it done on time. He'll think I'm lazy.*

Do you know for sure what the other person is thinking?   Yes   No

What else could the other person be thinking? Is this explanation more, equally, or less likely than your original thought? *He could understand that I was really sick, and since I was out for three days, he might realize that I honestly need the extension. This is probably just as likely if not more likely than my other thought since this teacher tends to be an understanding person.*

If the mind-reading thought turns out to be true (that is, the person tells you he or she is displeased with you), what can you do about it? *I could try to get it done quickly, or I could work with the teacher to make up my grade with another project.*

Now it's your turn:

Situation #1: _____

_____

Mind-reading thought: _____

_____

Do you know for sure what the other person is thinking?   Yes   No

What else could the person be thinking? Is this explanation more, equally, or less likely than your original thought?

_____

_____

_____

_____

If the mind-reading thought turns out to be true (that is, the person tells you he or she is displeased with you), what can you do about it?

_____

_____

Situation #2: _____

_____

Mind-reading thought: _____

_____

Do you know for sure what the other person is thinking?   Yes   No

What else could the person be thinking? Is this explanation more, equally, or less likely than your original thought?

_____

_____

_____

_____

If the mind-reading thought turns out to be true (that is, the person tells you he or she is displeased with you), what can you do about it?

_____

_____

To download another helpful exercise, please visit http://www.newharbinger.com /35845.

overresponsibility 7

for you to know

Overresponsibility is a kind of junk mail thought (that is, a distorted or unhelpful thought your worry sends you). It makes you believe you "should" do something in order to be a good person or that you have to take on all the responsibility to ensure that nothing bad happens. It's like a rule that your worry establishes for you. Consider these situations:

- Your club at school is planning a fund-raiser. Several members said they'd help the club officers by sitting for shifts at a fund-raising table in the cafeteria, but then these people bailed. Though you're not an officer, you worry that it'll be your fault if not enough money is raised, so you sign up for extra shifts. This cuts into time you need for studying.

- Your brother just started college in a city that has some areas of crime. You worry he doesn't know what he's getting into and think it's up to you to ensure his safety. You make a list of dangerous versus safe parts of the city and taxi/police numbers to put in his phone.

Overresponsibility is a distortion because it ignores other key aspects of the situation. Specifically, it may be that other people are actually responsible, or they may share the responsibility with you, like in the club fund-raising example. In other situations, what happens is not in your control. This lack of control may increase your anxiety so that you search for something—anything—you can do to feel more in control, like the example about your brother going to college. Overresponsibility leads you to expend a lot of effort trying to make things turn out okay when they would likely turn out okay anyway. This can take away from other important activities in your life or stress you out to the point that you're exhausted.

Lily is a high school senior who has her driver's license. Many of her friends don't have their licenses yet, so she often drives them around. It's gotten to the point that she spends hours a week driving her friends home from school, and to and from parties and other activities. Her gas costs are adding up. When she thinks about saying no to a friend who asks for a ride, she feels anxious. She thinks, *A good friend should always help out. Besides, they won't be able to go if I don't drive them.* She also imagines that she's keeping her friends safe by driving them home after late-night activities. After talking with her parents, though, she realizes that if she didn't have her license, her friends would still find some way to get around and it's ultimately their job to figure out how to do that. She practices telling her friends that she has too much going on when they ask her to drive them somewhere at an inconvenient time.

for you to do

Answer the following questions to help you determine the role overresponsibility plays in your life. Use the example below to guide you through the exercise:

1. Identify some part of your life for which you might take too much responsibility. What thoughts come up for you about this part of your life?

Two of my friends fight a lot and I end up in the middle. I worry they won't be friends anymore if I don't try to help them solve their problems, and then our group of friends won't be the same.

2. Who else (or what else) might also be responsible for this aspect of your life?

My two friends could work it out on their own—or another of our friends could help them.

3. How is your overresponsibility affecting your behavior? Is this getting in the way of your life at all?

I spend a lot of time talking to each of them, trying to figure out their problems. It really stresses me out and makes it hard for me to concentrate on other things I have to do.

4. Is it possible that this part of your life would work out fine if you decreased your responsibility by just 50 percent?

Yes, they could figure it out without my helping so much.

Now it's your turn:

1. Identify some part of your life for which you might take too much responsibility. What thoughts come up for you about this part of your life?

_____

_____

_____

2. Who else (or what else) might also be responsible for this aspect of your life?

_____

_____

_____

3. How is your overresponsibility affecting your behavior? Is this getting in the way of your life at all?

_____

_____

_____

4. Is it possible that this part of your life would work out fine if you decreased your responsibility by just 50 percent?

_____

_____

_____

more to do

Remember how Lily practiced telling her friends that she couldn't drive them around when she didn't have the time? This helped her to challenge her belief that she was responsible for their transportation. Other examples of tackling overresponsibility include these: if you're tempted to work extra shifts for the club fund-raiser, practice taking just *one* extra shift instead; or, if you feel you're responsible for your brother's safety at college, practice resisting the urge to point out the most recent crime that happened near his school.

Consider your answers to questions 3 and 4 in the first exercise, and identify one way that *you* could reduce your overresponsibility.

_____

_____

Now, pick a time to practice this over the next week. What happened when you reduced your responsibility?

_____

_____

8 intolerance of uncertainty

for you to know

Worriers like to know the exact details of what's going to happen. Their anxiety increases when a situation is unclear, or when there's more than one way the situation can turn out. In other words, they have trouble tolerating uncertainty. Uncertainty may cause a worried teen to leap to the worst-case scenario. Here are some examples:

- A teacher asks to meet after school ("I'm in trouble!")

- Test results are delayed after a doctor's visit ("I have a disease!")

- A friend isn't responding to a text ("He's mad at me!").

Some people hate uncertainty so much that they would prefer to know that something *bad* is going to happen so they can be prepared!

But life is often uncertain, with no clear-cut script describing what to do or what will happen next. This can be hard to accept, so you might do unhelpful and time-consuming things to try to gain certainty, without real success. For example, you may repeatedly ask your friends or parents if you're making the "correct" choice. Or, you may avoid situations—like trying out for a play or a sports team, pursuing a friendship, or applying to a "reach" or "magnet" school—if you don't know how they'll turn out or if you'll be successful. Such intolerance of uncertainty can really get in the way of life. Accepting that uncertainty is a part of life definitely takes practice, but as you gain confidence that you can handle what happens without advance notice (and that what happens usually isn't bad!), your anxiety will decrease.

James is a fourteen-year-old who worries a lot about his school performance and whether he's making good decisions. He thinks that he gets good grades only because he painstakingly plans out when he'll do his homework. He writes long lists and overly detailed schedules (which take a lot of time) and repeatedly asks his teachers about upcoming assignments to make sure he understands correctly what's expected of him. However, he gets very anxious when things don't go as he planned. He avoided going to math class one day because there was a substitute teacher, and he sometimes has panic attacks when he doesn't finish work according to his strict schedule (even if it's still before the deadline). James also struggles with making decisions. His parents asked him to pick a summer camp, and even after several hours of online research, he pleaded with his parents to make the decision for him so it wouldn't be his fault if he made the "wrong" choice.

James recently started working with a cognitive behavioral therapist who has encouraged him to test out what would happen if he made gradually less detailed plans and if he made a decision without checking with his parents first. For example, though he still had a long list of homework assignments to complete, he refrained from making a minute-by-minute schedule of when he would get everything done. Although initially anxious, with experience James has become more confident that things will turn out okay even without all his planning and checking, which has led to less worry overall.

James completed a worksheet that was especially helpful in reducing his anxiety about not having a detailed schedule:

List all of the anxious thoughts you had about this situation.

I'm not going to get everything done without a schedule.

I won't know what I should do first.

I'll feel too uncomfortable without having a plan.

What actually happened?

I got all my homework done and still had time left over.

It didn't end up mattering what I did first.

I was uncomfortable, but I was still able to do my work.

Compare what actually happened to what you feared would happen. Did your predictions come true?

No, they didn't come true. I was able to do what I needed to without a long schedule.

How well did you deal with what actually happened in the situation?

I was less anxious than I thought I'd be.

for you to do

Like James, identify a situation you've encountered in the past few weeks that made you worry because you didn't know how it was going to turn out (for example, waiting for your parents to decide if they'd allow you to go to a party, trying an activity for the first time, or waiting for the results of a test).

List all of the anxious thoughts you had about this situation.

_____

_____

_____

What actually happened?

_____

_____

Compare what actually happened to what you feared would happen. Did your predictions come true?

_____

_____

How well did you deal with what actually happened in the situation?

_____

_____

To download another helpful exercise, please visit http://www.newharbinger.com /35845.

Dealing with Worry Thoughts

9 ignoring unhelpful thoughts

for you to know

Imagine that your mom asks you to get the mail. You bring it in and notice a bright pink flyer that says, "Congratulations—you've won a free cruise! Call us at 1–888-UR-PRIZE to claim your trip!" Knowing it's unlikely you've actually won a fantastic cruise, you probably throw the flyer away, right? You easily recognize the flyer as junk mail.

Recall from prior activities that many worry thoughts are like junk mail. They are unhelpful distortions that keep you from considering all possible interpretations of the situation:

- black-and-white thinking (making judgments at one extreme or the other without thinking of the "middle ground")

- catastrophizing (thinking the worst-case scenario will happen and you'll be helpless to deal with it)

- mind reading (believing you know what others are thinking about you)

- overresponsibility (putting too much pressure on yourself to prevent bad things from happening)

- intolerance of uncertainty (trying to predict what will happen in a situation when you can't actually make a prediction)

Paying attention to junk mail thoughts is like keeping the cruise flyer and calling to claim your prize—a waste of your time and energy. Just like tossing the flyer, imagine that you can "throw away" a junk mail thought whenever it pops into your head. Indeed, with practice, you can learn to ignore such unhelpful thinking!

Celeste is a talented performer who has had several starring roles in musicals at her school. She hopes to major in theater in college. Despite positive feedback from her drama teachers and directors, she's always very anxious before a performance. She has a lot of automatic and unhelpful thoughts, like *I'm going to mess up; I'm okay, but I'll never be good enough to get into musical theater programs;* and *My director probably thinks I'm not working hard enough.* She learns to pay close attention to the thoughts as they come into her mind and to label the unhelpful ones as junk mail. For example, when she catches herself worrying that her director is judging her negatively, she talks back to the thought by saying, "There I go again with the mind reading. How can I possibly know what she's thinking?" Celeste tells herself that the thought is a waste of time and imagines tossing it into the garbage. The thought pops up again (many times), but as she repeatedly acknowledges it as junk mail and practices "throwing it away," she's able to dismiss it almost immediately, and the thought gradually becomes less frequent.

for you to do

Before you learn how to ignore your junk mail thinking, it helps to practice identifying and labeling your unhelpful thinking patterns.

Identify a situation that triggers your worry thoughts. (It might help to keep a list of these situations in your phone or on a scrap of paper over the course of the week to use in this exercise; you can also refer back to the chart in Activity 3). Then, write down every anxious thought you have about the situation:

_____

_____

_____

Look at the thoughts above. Are they helping you in any way? If not, determine if any of those thoughts are junk mail thoughts and circle the type(s) of junk mail below:

black-and-white thinking

catastrophizing

mind reading

overresponsibility

intolerance of uncertainty

Just like when Celeste caught herself "mind reading," tell yourself that your unhelpful worry thought is the type of junk mail that you circled. For example, if you're worried about blanking out on a test, you can say to yourself, *I'm catastrophizing again.* If you think that you failed because you got a B on a paper, you can say to yourself, *There's my black-and-white thinking talking.*

more to do

Now that you've practiced identifying and labeling your junk mail thoughts, it's time to learn how to ignore the thoughts when they come up again. Select one of your worry thoughts from the first exercise and write it here:

_____

How often does the thought come into your mind on a scale from   _____
0 (never) to 10 (all the time)?

How anxious does the thought make you feel on a scale from   _____
0 (not at all) to 10 (extremely anxious)?

Now, just like throwing away an actual piece of junk mail, imagine throwing your unhelpful thought into the garbage. The first time you do this, it may help to write the thought down on paper, crumple it up, and throw it away. Thereafter, visualize throwing the thought away while saying to yourself, *This thought isn't worth my time* or *I don't need to pay attention to this*. Be consistent: repeat this exercise whenever the thought pops into your head again, even if you have to ignore it dozens of times. After a week or two of practice, rerate the following:

How often does the thought come into your mind on a scale from   _____
0 (never) to 10 (all the time)?

How anxious does the thought make you feel on a scale from   _____
0 (not at all) to 10 (extremely anxious)?

How has acknowledging and then ignoring the unhelpful thought changed its frequency and how anxious it makes you feel?

_____

_____

10 taking the sting out of worry thoughts

for you to know

When you're worried, your anxious thoughts seem very real and believable. Your worries repeat over and over, and with repetition, you unwittingly train yourself to react with an intense burst of anxiety whenever a particular worry thought shows up again. However, just because you're having a worry doesn't mean you have to *believe* it or that you have to be stuck to it like glue. The thoughts are just thoughts and not necessarily *The Truth*. With practice, you can become a more detached observer (rather than a victim) of your worry thoughts. The developers of acceptance and commitment therapy (ACT; Hayes, Strosahl, and Wilson 1999) call this process "cognitive defusion," or unsticking yourself from unhelpful thoughts. This distances you from those thoughts, allowing you to consider them more objectively. With distance also comes a reduction in the intensity, or "sting," of anxiety associated with the thoughts.

One basic cognitive defusion strategy is to clearly describe your worry as "having a thought." For example, if you're anxious about flying on a plane and think, *The plane is going to crash!*, try restating it as *I'm having a thought that the plane is going to crash.* Similarly, if you worry, *I'm going to fail my exam,* tell yourself instead, *My mind is telling me that I'm going to fail.* Restating your worries in this way subtly reminds you that there may be other ways to think about the situation.

Seventeen-year-old Olivia will start college in a few months. She isn't comfortable with unfamiliar situations and has been having a lot of worries about college. A stream of worries—like *My roommate will hate me; I won't be able to handle college work;* and, *I won't be as close with my high school friends anymore*—frequently flow through her mind. If she considers each thought to be the truth, she becomes increasingly anxious. However, she's been working on labeling her worries as "just thoughts." For example, she restates her worries as *I'm having the thought that my roommate will hate me* or *My mind is telling me I won't be able to handle college work.* By restating her worries this way, she notices that they don't seem so big and overwhelming. Rather, each thought seems like just one way (of many) that she can think about the situation. She's also found that her worries seem much less real and threatening when she says them in a funny voice. For example, imagine her saying, "My roommate will hate me" in a high-pitched chipmunk voice! It may be a little silly, but the more she distances herself from her worry thoughts in these ways, the less panicky she feels when they pop into her head.

for you to do

This exercise will help you practice labeling your worry as "just a thought" rather than as the definite truth. See Olivia's case (above) for some examples.

Write down a worry that has been bothering you lately.

_____

_____

Restate the worry in the following ways:

I'm having the thought that _____

_____

My mind is telling me that _____

_____

Continue to rephrase the worry every time it comes into your mind this week. Is there any difference in how anxious you feel when you restate your worry as "having a thought"?

_____

_____

more to do

Another cognitive defusion strategy used in ACT (Hayes, Strosahl, and Wilson 1999) involves singing your worry out loud or saying it in a funny voice (like Olivia did).

Write down another worry that has been bothering you.

_____

_____

Now, try singing the worry again and again to the tune of a familiar song. For example, imagine singing "Fail, fail, I'm going to fail" to the tune of "Row, Row, Row Your Boat." Is doing this kind of ridiculous? Yes, it is. But you'll laugh while you're doing it, and it's hard to take a worry too seriously if you're laughing at the same time!

If singing just isn't your thing, say the worry in a funny voice instead. Try a high- or low-pitched voice, or the voice of your favorite superhero. Another option if you have a smartphone is to try one of the many "voice changer" applications available—it will "say" your worry in a funny voice for you.

11 challenging worry thoughts

for you to know

Although your first line of defense when dealing with worry thoughts is to try to acknowledge and ignore them (Activity 9) or give yourself some distance from them (Activity 10), some worries are especially persistent and need to be challenged directly through a process called "cognitive restructuring." *Cognitive restructuring* is a fancy name for challenging your thoughts by examining the evidence for and against them, like detectives do when gathering clues to prove or disprove their theory of a case.

In other words, treat your worry thought as just one possibility to be evaluated. Look at the arguments for and against your thought by asking yourself some key questions:

- *What has happened in a similar situation in the past?*

- *Do I know 100 percent that what I'm worried about will happen?*

- *What's the worst that can happen? Can I deal with that?*

- *Is there a more likely, positive way the situation can turn out?*

- *What would I tell a friend if he or she were worried about this?*

- *Do I have any other evidence that this thought is untrue?*

Not every question will be appropriate for all worry thoughts. For example, if you're worried about a catastrophe (like your plane crashing), then asking yourself *Can I deal with that?* is probably unhelpful! Instead, select the questions that are best suited to your particular worry thought, and then use your answers to draw a conclusion about whether your worry is supported by the evidence. When there's not much evidence to support your worry, you can generate a *rational response*, or a counterthought that directly challenges the worry thought.

See how cognitive restructuring works for Jackson, a thirteen-year-old boy who's allergic to peanuts. If he eats peanuts, he experiences a non-life-threatening reaction that causes him to break out in hives and to wheeze. Though he's typically very careful not to eat foods that contain peanuts, once when he was in the fifth grade, he accidentally ate some ice cream that had peanuts in it and had to go to the emergency room for an allergic reaction. Since then, he's been very worried about eating anything prepared outside of his home, even when assured that the food is peanut-free. Sometimes he convinces himself he's having a reaction when he isn't—instead, he's having panicky physical feelings (like his heart beating faster) that he confuses with an allergic reaction. Jackson has had so many false alarms that he's been working with a therapist to practice challenging his worries about having an allergic reaction by answering the following questions:

What has happened in a similar situation in the past?

There have been many times when I thought I was having an allergic reaction when it turned out I was just anxious. In the past five years, only one time out of about one hundred did I actually have a reaction—that's only 1 percent of the time.

What's the worst that can happen? Can I deal with that?

My allergy isn't life threatening. The worst that can happen is that I feel really uncomfortable and have to go to the ER for steroids. That isn't fun, but I can definitely handle it.

Is there a more likely, positive way the situation can turn out?

Yes—it's most likely I'm not having a reaction and I'll be fine.

Based on this evidence, Jackson's therapist asks him to write down a rational response, or something he can tell himself, to challenge his worry the next time it pops up. He writes, "I'm careful about what I eat, so it's very unlikely I'll have an allergic reaction. But if worse comes to worst, I can deal with having a reaction and getting treatment for it."

for you to do

Practice challenging your own worry thoughts. First, write down a recent worry that has been persistently bothering you.

_____

_____

Next, put a star next to the questions below that most apply to your worry thought. Answer those questions as best you can.

What has happened in a similar situation in the past?

_____

_____

Do I know 100 percent that what I'm worried about will happen?

_____

_____

What's the worst that can happen? Can I deal with that?

_____

_____

Is there a more likely, positive way the situation can turn out?

_____

_____

What would I tell a friend if he or she were worried about this?

_____

_____

Do I have any other evidence that this thought is untrue?

_____

_____

more to do

Review your answers to the questions above. Based on your evidence, practice coming up with two different rational responses (or statements you can say to yourself) that directly challenge your worry thought. If you get stuck, it can help to focus on the advice you'd give your friend if he or she had the same worry.

1. _____

_____

2. _____

_____

Challenging worry thoughts can be difficult if you have the belief that worry is somehow protective or leads to good things happening. For help addressing this belief (and for more practice challenging thoughts), please see Activity 28 (Stop Giving Worry So Much Credit) at http://www.newharbinger.com/35845.

putting a halt to worry hopping 12

David, a fourteen-year-old ninth grader, is having trouble falling asleep. He's been lying awake for an hour, his mind racing as he feels increasingly anxious. When he first went to bed, he started thinking about his geometry test the next day: *I probably should have studied more. I might not do well.* He then remembered that he also has a Spanish presentation later in the week and he hasn't started it yet. He hears a noise somewhere else in the house and thinks, *Could someone be breaking in?* His friend Mike had a break-in at his house a few years ago. Mike goes to a different school, and suddenly David wonders, *Is Mike mad at me? I can't remember if I messaged him back last week—maybe he thinks I'm ditching him.* He jumps from worry to worry until he gets tired enough to stop thinking and go to sleep.

for you to know

David's experience trying to fall asleep is a classic example of "worry hopping." *Worry hopping* involves jumping rapidly from one worry to the next without ever resolving any of the worry thoughts that come up. Worry hopping is a subtle strategy for avoiding feelings of anxiety. To illustrate, when you go from Worry A to Worry B, you're avoiding whatever anxiety Worry A brought up for you. Worry C then distracts you from anxiety associated with Worry B, and so on. When you're really worried about a particular situation, it's not uncommon to avoid thinking about it by worrying about something a little less scary. For example, David was most anxious about his geometry test, so thinking about his Spanish presentation took his mind off the biggest worry (even though the Spanish presentation was also worrisome). In addition, worry hopping keeps you stuck in the future or in the past, distracting you from the here and now (in David's case, trying to fall asleep).

This activity will help you identify your own patterns of worry hopping, after which you'll learn to experience your most anxiety-provoking worry without avoiding it. Later sections of this book provide additional strategies to halt worry hopping— see in particular Activity 13 (Staying in the Moment) and Activity 14 (Facing Feared Situations).

for you to do

Over the next week, notice times when you feel especially frantic and anxious. It might feel like your mind races from one worry thought to another. As soon as you can, write down every worry thought that's swirling around in your head. If it's easier, record the thoughts on a scrap of paper or on your phone or computer. For example, David wrote:

I probably should have studied more. I might not do well. I could get a bad grade this quarter in geometry.

Ugh, I have my Spanish presentation later this week, too. I'm totally not ready.

What was that noise—could someone be breaking in? Mike had that happen to him. I don't think anyone was home when it happened.

Is Mike mad at me? I can't remember if I messaged him back last week—maybe he thinks I'm ditching him.

Write your own experience with worry hopping here:

Worry Thought 1: _____

_____

Worry Thought 2: _____

_____

Worry Thought 3: _____

_____

Worry Thought 4: _____

_____

more to do

Take a look at your list in the first exercise. Rate the level of anxiety that comes up for you when you think about each worry, using a scale from 0 (not at all anxiety provoking) to 10 (extremely anxiety provoking). Circle the worry that you gave the highest number.

This exercise encourages you to experience the thoughts and feelings associated with your most anxiety-provoking worry. As you focus on the worry, think about what bothers you the most about the situation. Allow yourself to imagine that aspect of the worry again and again without avoiding it—try this for five to ten minutes, if possible. If your mind starts to drift to other topics, gently pull your attention back to the thoughts and feelings associated with this worry. You may notice that your anxiety rating increases at first (it will feel uncomfortable), but as you sit with the worry and stay focused on the parts that bother you, your anxiety rating will likely start to decrease. Stick with it—the purpose of the exercise is to get used to the worry to the point that it isn't so threatening the next time it pops up.

Here's how David completed the exercise:

Write down the most anxiety-provoking worry thought from your list.

I probably should have studied more. I might not do well. I could get a bad grade this quarter in geometry.

What bothers you the most about your worry thought?

My teacher and my parents will be disappointed that I didn't give my best effort.

Stay focused on the aspect of your worry that bothers you the most. Imagine it in as much detail as possible. How anxiety provoking is this image when you first think of it (0–10)?

8. (David imagines his parents shaking their heads as they see his quarter grades; he also pictures his teacher telling him he needs to try harder.)

Continue to imagine the most bothersome aspect of your worry for five to ten minutes. How anxiety provoking is the image now (0–10)?

3. It really isn't bothering me that much anymore.

Now you try it:

Write down the most anxiety-provoking worry thought from your list:

_____

_____

What bothers you the most about this worry thought?

_____

_____

Stay focused on the aspect of your worry that bothers you the most. Imagine it in as much detail as possible. How anxiety provoking is this image when you first think of it (0–10)?

_____

Continue to imagine the most bothersome aspect of your worry for five to ten minutes. How anxiety provoking is the image now (0–10)?

_____

13 staying in the moment

for you to know

By definition, worry focuses on the future—"What's going to happen next? What could go wrong? What if...?" Worriers also tend to ruminate (or obsess) about the past and wonder if they could have done something differently. Such emphasis on the future and the past, which has been shown to increase stress, keeps worriers from being able to concentrate on what's happening *now*. Further, because people who worry often take on many different responsibilities, they try to do more than one thing at a time (for example, completing a math assignment while sitting in on a play rehearsal as a friend whispers something in their ear). Such multitasking seems efficient, but it actually leads to making more mistakes and feeling burned out. Why? Because every time you turn your attention away from a task to focus on another one, you have to reorient yourself to the first task (over and over again).

The antidote is something called *mindfulness*, a process that involves paying attention to the present moment by taking it in with all five of your senses. (You get bonus points if you objectively observe the moment without judgment!) Even five minutes a day of staying in the moment can help to reduce stress; in fact, regularly practicing mindfulness has been shown to reduce physical symptoms of stress and improve self-esteem in teens with anxiety and depression (Biegel et al. 2009). It can be hard at first to keep your mind focused on just one aspect of the present—you have to gently and repeatedly bring your mind back to the task at hand—but it gets easier with practice.

Veronica is a tenth grader who describes herself as "always focused on the 'what ifs' in life." She tries to imagine every way that a situation can turn out and how she'll deal with each outcome. Not only that, but she tries to anticipate potential problems and stop them before they arise. For example, she makes sure she sees each of her friends an equal amount so no one can be upset with her for playing favorites. Veronica is so caught up in her head all the time that it's hard for her to stay focused on what's happening now. Once, it took her an hour longer than it normally would to finish a math assignment because she couldn't stop checking her phone for messages. She also has trouble enjoying herself when spending time with friends and family because she's always thinking about what's coming next and what she still needs to do. Recently, her guidance counselor has been helping her stay more aware of the moment by closely paying attention to her surroundings and describing to herself what she observes. For instance, she's been taking a walk with her dog every night and using that time to really notice the rustling of leaves in the trees as well as the smell of the fresh air and the feel of the sidewalk underneath her feet. Veronica has noticed that being just a little more mindful has helped her feel less frenzied.

for you to do

This first exercise is an example of mindfulness meditation—it involves taking a "time-out" for five minutes to completely focus on your internal experience. This might feel scary for some who are used to a lot of activity or distraction, so if five minutes feels overwhelming, start with one minute and see if you can gradually increase the amount of time over the course of a few days.

> *Find a comfortable chair to sit where you're unlikely to be interrupted (yes, that means turning your phone off or putting it away). If you're comfortable doing so, close your eyes. Take one slow deep breath—your belly, not your chest, should rise and fall as you breathe to ensure you're breathing in a way that's relaxing. Feel the chair beneath you as it supports your body. As you slowly take your next breath, silently count "one," and as you breathe out, count "two." Inhale "three," exhale "four," inhale "five," exhale "six," and so on until you reach ten. Once you reach ten, start to count backward as you breathe—inhale "ten," exhale "nine," inhale "eight," continuing until you get back to one. When you get to one, do it all over again, counting all the way up to ten and back to one. As you complete this exercise, your job is to keep your mind focused on counting your breaths. This is easier said than done, so when your thoughts start to drift away, no big deal—just gently bring them back to the exercise, even if you have to do this many times. If you lose count of your breaths, or if you accidentally count higher than ten, start the exercise over again.*

Complete this mindfulness practice every day for the next week, ideally for five minutes at a time, keeping track in the chart that follows. To download blank copies of this chart, please visit http://www.newharbinger.com/35845.

Day	Practiced mindfulness— Yes/No? How long?	What did you notice while doing the exercise?
Example: Monday	Yes, six minutes	It was challenging to stay focused at first, but got a little easier by the end.

more to do

Another way to practice mindfulness is to pick a moment—any moment—in your day to fully engage in what you're doing and pay attention to your experience using all five of your senses. A good (and delicious) way to learn how to do this is to mindfully make a batch of chocolate chip cookies while staying completely immersed in the task at hand. As you make the cookies, notice the little dots of chocolate as you mix them into the sticky batter, feel the tension of the spoon against the batter as you mix, hear the slight sizzle as the cookies bake in the oven, smell the mouthwatering aroma of baking cookies, and, finally, taste the warm, gooey chocolate chip cookie as soon as it's done baking.

Whatever activity you decide to do mindfully, to get the most out of your experience, do your best to stay focused on your sensations and, again, gently bring your thoughts back to what you're doing if you notice your mind drifts. Don't try to do more than one activity at a time—for instance, don't mindfully bake cookies while watching a video on your computer. One thing at a time.

Practice mindfully engaging in one activity per day. If you're stuck for ideas, try practicing mindfulness while (a) eating a snack or a piece of candy, (b) taking a walk outside, (c) playing catch or shooting hoops with a friend, or (d) working on a piece of art. Record your observations in the chart below. To download blank copies of this chart, please visit http://www.newharbinger.com/35845.

Day	What activity did you complete mindfully?	Describe your experience
Example: *Saturday*	*While babysitting my little sister, we made things out of clay.*	*The clay was soft and pliable, and the colors kind of mixed together as we made a little bowl. I got a text and was tempted to check it, but I kept the phone in my bag and focused on how the clay felt in my hands.*

Changing Unhelpful Behavior

14 facing feared situations

for you to know

When you predict something negative will happen in a situation (as many worriers do), it's understandable that you might start avoiding it as much as possible. For example, if you worry you'll mess up when you participate in class, you might decide not to participate at all. If you worry that new people won't like you, you may avoid places where you have to interact with someone new. Or, if you worry about getting a dental exam, you might put off going to see the dentist. The tendency to avoid situations that make you feel anxious is completely understandable—avoidance leads to immediate relief, at least in the short term, and it's hard to stop doing something that makes you feel better so quickly and effectively.

The problem is that avoidance doesn't work well in the long term, especially if you must face the situation eventually. When you avoid an anxiety-provoking situation, you can't test out if what you fear will actually happen. You assume the worst, which makes the avoided situation seem scarier and scarier. For example, if you don't participate in class, you never have the chance to see that your teacher or peers may actually appreciate what you have to say (or at the least, that no one harshly judges you). If you avoid going to the dentist, you never get a chance to see that the exam is probably not as bad as you imagined.

Avoidance is particularly unhelpful when it keeps you from taking part in social, academic, extracurricular, or family activities that you *want* to be doing. All the same, you may be thinking, *There's no way I can simply face my worst fears, just like that.* Well, you certainly don't have to learn to face feared situations by doing the hardest thing first. Just like a kid learning to swim in a pool, you can start by wading into the shallow end first before you dive headfirst into the deep end. This strategy is called *gradual exposure,* and it reduces avoidance by having you face the "least feared" situations first, and then working your way up to the "most feared." In this way, exposure is a manageable process. Indeed, exposure is the most powerful approach to long-term anxiety reduction.

Joe is an eighth grader who lives with his mom and older brother. His older brother got a part-time job recently, so he isn't home much. Joe worries a lot about safety issues, and has been reluctant to stay home by himself when his mom's at work or running errands; he's worried someone might break into the house or kidnap him, though his neighborhood is pretty safe. Whenever he does stay at home for even short periods of time, he tends to call his mom often to ask when she's coming home, and he repeatedly checks to make sure the doors are locked. He's been going to his grandma's house after school, but Joe wishes he could be more independent. He especially wants to be able to stay home by himself after school so he can get a head start on his homework before his mom gets home.

Joe starts working with a therapist who helps him develop a gradual plan to reach the goal of staying home alone after school and on weekends when his mom has to run to the store. They make a hierarchy of situations (see below), ranking them based on how anxiety provoking each would be for Joe. The hardest situation (the goal) is at the top of the hierarchy, followed by the next hardest situation, and so on. The most manageable situation is on the bottom.

Situation	Fear rating (0–10)
Stay home alone for two hours without checking the locks and without calling Mom or Grandma for nonemergencies.	9
Stay home alone for two hours; can check locks once and call Mom or Grandma once.	7
Stay home alone for one hour without checking the locks and without calling Mom or Grandma for nonemergencies.	6
Stay home alone for one hour; can check locks once and call Mom or Grandma once.	5
Stay home alone for thirty minutes without checking locks or calling Mom for nonemergencies while she runs to the store.	5
Stay home alone for thirty minutes while Mom runs to the store; can check locks once and call once.	4
Stay home alone for fifteen minutes while Mom takes a walk around the block.	3

Joe's willing to try the lowest item on his list first, since he rated it as mildly anxiety provoking. After practicing that situation a few times, he's ready to move on to the next item. He finds that it isn't easy—he has to let himself experience feelings of anxiety, which can sometimes be intense. But he keeps working his way up the hierarchy, finding that with lots of practice, his anxiety becomes less intense and decreases more rapidly. By the time he gets to his goal item (staying home alone for two hours after school without calling his mom or checking the locks), he's less anxious and more confident than he expected to be when he first made the list. With experience, he realizes that "nothing bad has happened," and he reaches the point of being able to stay home alone whenever he needs to.

for you to do

Select a situation you've been avoiding because of your anxiety. If you're having trouble picking a situation, consider these examples:

- auditioning for a play or trying out for a team

- answering questions in class

- asking a friend to hang out

- going on a sleepover or an overnight trip

- introducing yourself to a group of new people

- trying out a new activity

Try starting with a situation that you really want to be able to do. The motivation will help keep you going during the challenge.

Next, just like Joe did, write the ultimate goal at the top of the list and rate how anxiety provoking this would be for you if you did it right now (from 0 = no anxiety to 10 = very high anxiety). From there, come up with ways the situation could become less anxiety provoking, write them down, and then order the list from most to least scary. Joe and his therapist made his situation easier by allowing him to check the locks and call his loved ones; they also decreased the amount of time he had to be in the situation. If your ultimate goal is to try out for a sports team, lower items on the hierarchy might include practicing the sport with one or two friends, playing for fun with a larger group of friends, and/or trying out for a more casual team (like a low-pressure town league or intramural team). For more sample exposure hierarchies, please visit http://www.newharbinger.com/35845.

Situation	Fear rating (0–10)

Now, just like Joe did, start working toward your goal by trying the lowest item on your list first. After you do that a few times, move up to the next item. Keep going until you reach your goal. Remember: *you will feel anxious doing this, and that's okay.* Your job is to experience the anxiety *and* stick with it anyway, keeping in mind that it will very likely get easier the more you practice.

To download another helpful exercise, please visit http://www.newharbinger.com /35845.

testing your hypotheses 15

for you to know

You may remember learning in science class how to test hypotheses. A *hypothesis* is a prediction or guess about what will happen as a result of an experiment. For example, you might hypothesize that new trees that are watered twice a week will grow taller than trees watered once a month (too little) or multiple times a day (too much). Your worry also comes up with hypotheses about what will happen in stressful situations: you predict that you'll fail your chemistry test if you don't study a whole week in advance, that your best friend will be mad at you if you don't return her text right away, or that you'll get lost if you go somewhere new. Unless you actually face the situation you're worried about without using a *safety behavior*—doing something unnecessary or excessive to prevent something bad from happening—or without avoiding it altogether, you aren't fully testing whether your prediction will come true. Here, you'll learn how to keep track of what really happens in stressful or worrisome situations when you don't avoid them. Over time, you'll start to notice patterns that help you determine if your worry's predictions come true or if they tend to be false.

Jake is a baseball player who worries he isn't gaining the skill he needs to keep playing on his school team. He's had a slump recently, with his batting average down to about .200. Until now, he's tried to feel less worried by spending many hours at batting practice and extra time in the weight room to get ready for games. His coach has commented that his preparations are overkill, and that Jake might actually hit better if he weren't overtaxing his body. Jake isn't convinced, but agrees to test out his coach's hypothesis. He keeps track of his batting practice time, weight room time, and number of hits at games each week for a month.

Week of:	Number of minutes in batting practice	Number of minutes in weight room	Number of games this week	Hits/at bats
April 4	185	130	2	2/8 (.250)
April 11	150	75	2	3/7 (.429)
April 18	120	60	3	4/10 (.400)
April 25	115	60	2	4/9 (.444)

Jake takes a look at his chart and recognizes that his coach's prediction came true—less time spent in extra batting practice and weight room sessions led to an overall improvement in his batting average. This directly challenges his worry that he isn't working hard enough to stay on the team. (In fact, he may have been working too hard.)

for you to do

As you're learning to test out your worry thoughts, it may be helpful to start with a one-time, straightforward experiment. Here are some examples:

- Scott worries that if he returns a shirt he bought to the store, the person working the register will question him or otherwise give him a hard time. He tests out this hypothesis by returning the shirt and seeing what happens. The store clerk just processes the transaction without asking Scott anything about it.

- Aly thinks she'll never be able to fall asleep if she goes to a sleepover at her friend's house. She agrees to go and observes that, although it took her a little longer than usual, she was able to fall asleep eventually.

- Pete imagines that if he raises his hand to answer a question in class, he'll get the answer wrong and his classmates will laugh. He decides to try to answer several questions in his math class today. He gets two of the three answers correct. He gets one answer wrong, but when he looks around the class, no one seems to care (and no one laughs).

What is a one-time experiment you can conduct to test out something you have been worried about? _____

What is the hypothesis you'll be testing out? _____

_____

Select a time to conduct the experiment. _____

How did it go? Did your prediction come true? _____

_____

more to do

This exercise will look at evidence for and against your hypotheses (or predictions) over time. Over the next week or two, write down all the upcoming situations you're worried about. Then, write down your predictions for each situation. Do your best not to avoid any aspect of the situation (see Activity 16 for further information on unhelpful behaviors). Next, write down what actually happened. To download blank copies of this chart, please visit http://www.newharbinger.com/35845.

Date	Situation	Prediction	What actually happened
Example: *August 9*	*Emma's birthday party at the beach*	*No one will talk to me at the party. I'll stand in a corner by myself the whole time.*	*I tried not to stay in the corner. A few people from school started talking to me, and we ended up playing volleyball together.*

Overall, how often did your predictions come true? Can you draw any conclusions from the information you collected here?

_____

_____

_____

If any of your worries did come true, was the outcome as bad as you imagined? How did you cope with it?

_____

_____

_____

16 identifying safety behaviors

for you to know

In Activity 14, we talked about how many worriers completely avoid situations that make them feel anxious. However, avoidance isn't always so clear-cut. Sometimes people still participate in a situation that makes them feel worried, but they take specific actions they believe will protect them from something bad happening. These actions are called *safety behaviors*. Safety behaviors tend to be excessive, time consuming, and energy draining. Just like avoiding a situation altogether, you may believe that something bad will happen if you stop engaging in the safety behavior; the more you use the safety behavior, the stronger your belief that the bad thing will happen.

Safety behaviors are subtle forms of avoidance, and thus are tricky to identify. In small doses, the behaviors can be normal and understandable, but they likely cross into safety behavior territory if one or more of the following is true:

- The behaviors are objectively unnecessary. They are actions you take to try to ward off a threat when the threat is pretty unlikely (or else would be manageable if it occurred).

- The behaviors occur frequently (in some cases, many times a day), so they take up a lot of time and energy.

- You would feel anxious if you didn't engage in the behaviors.

There are many different types of safety behaviors, but those below are the most common among teen worriers. (Later activities will discuss each in more detail.)

Reassurance-seeking and checking: These safety behaviors are often used in response to fear of making mistakes or fear of the unknown. Though it's normal to sometimes ask others for their opinions or to double-check that you've done or understood something correctly, some worried teens *repeatedly* and *excessively* ask others (often parents, teachers, or friends) for reassurance about minor matters. Others might ask the same question over and over, even when they're pretty sure they know the answer.

People pleasing: This is common among those who worry they'll disappoint or anger other people. While it's important to be nice to others and treat them well, people pleasing becomes a safety behavior when you do things to make others happy at the expense of what's best for you—this means you tend not to assert yourself.

Overpreparing: Teens who worry a lot about performing poorly in school or extracurricular activities may overprepare. Examples include studying more than needed to do well on a test, writing multiple drafts of an essay when two drafts would have been sufficient, and writing down every little thing the teacher says because *"What if it ends up being important?".*

Distraction and procrastination: Some worried teens use distraction (for example, playing video games to avoid thinking about a tough homework assignment) to avoid having anxious thoughts and feelings. Procrastination involves putting off a challenging task because of the discomfort the task provokes.

It's not uncommon for worried teens to use more than one type of safety behavior. Consider Alicia, who engages in all of the safety behaviors reviewed above. She's a high school student who has worried about her grades for as long as she can remember. Before high school, she often did more work than was required (for example, doing extra math problems or writing longer reports and essays), and she rewrote her notes if they looked messy. She hoped that her teachers would notice her hard work and be pleased she cared so much about school. Now that she's in high school, she's still driven to "go above and beyond," but it's much harder given the increased workload. When she has an upcoming test, she asks her parents repeatedly if they think she's studied enough. When they reassure her that she knows the material well, she feels better for a few minutes but then starts to doubt whether that's really true, causing her to review her notes all over again. Her teachers have also told her that she'd likely do just as well in school if she cut her work time, but Alicia thinks this is too risky to try (*What if I start getting bad grades?*). Her tendency to overprepare and check in with her parents/teachers about the quality of her work has become exhausting. Lately, Alicia has started to put off doing her work: "I don't have the energy to do what I need to do right now." The more she procrastinates (and the further behind she gets), the more anxious she feels.

for you to do

This activity will help you figure out if you use any unhelpful safety behaviors. Examine the list below and put a check by any behaviors you use *frequently* or *excessively* to try to prevent something bad from happening (or to keep yourself from feeling anxious). Hint: If it would make you feel anxious to not engage in the behavior, it's probably a safety behavior.

The checklist is organized by type of safety behavior as described above: reassurance-seeking and checking, people pleasing, overpreparing, and distraction/ procrastination. If you have checked off one or more safety behaviors per category, make sure to read the activity later in this book that corresponds with that type of safety behavior.

Reassurance-Seeking and Checking (Activity 17)

☐ When I have to make even small decisions, I often ask my parents or friends what they think I should do.

☐ I often ask my parents, teachers, or friends if they think I've done something correctly.

☐ I often ask people if they're mad at me.

☐ I ask the same question multiple times.

☐ When I'm worried, I frequently check the Internet for information that'll make me feel better.

☐ Even when I'm pretty sure I've done something okay, I double-check (or triple-check) to make sure I'm not mistaken.

People Pleasing (Activity 18)

☐ I go out of my way to make sure people don't get upset with me.

☐ I avoid telling people when their behavior bothers me.

☐ I don't usually tell people that I disagree with them.

☐ I tend to choose classes or activities that others want me to do (which aren't always the ones I want to do).

Overpreparing (Activity 19)

☐ I often spend more time studying for tests or quizzes than is necessary.

☐ I try to write down everything my teachers say so I don't miss anything.

☐ I rehearse presentations or performances much more than other people do.

☐ I push myself to the point of exhaustion in academics, sports, or other extracurricular activities.

Distraction and Procrastination (Activity 20)

☐ When I have something challenging to do, I tend to put it off and do something else instead.

☐ When I'm faced with something that makes me feel uncomfortable, I avoid it by distracting myself (for example, watching videos or TV, playing video games, going on social media, and so on).

☐ I often wait until the last minute to get started on tough assignments.

☐ When I have a list of things to do, I usually do the easiest things first, even if they're less important.

more to do

Monitoring your behavior is often the first step toward changing your behavior. Of the safety behaviors you checked off above, pick one category that most interferes with your life (that is, takes up your time and energy at school, with friends, and at home). Over the next week, pay close attention to when you use this safety behavior, recording specific examples in the chart below (see Alicia's example at the top), or noting them in your phone or computer. To download blank copies of this chart, please visit http://www.newharbinger.com/35845.

Day	Situation	Safety behavior
Example: *Sunday*	*I have a test tomorrow*	*I keep going over my notes long after I've really understood the material.*

reducing reassurance-seeking and checking 17

Riley is a seventh grader who frequently doubts if she's done something correctly or made the right decision. She also worries a lot about health and safety issues—the possibility that she or her parents have a disease, her family will get into a car accident, or someone will kidnap her. She hates not knowing for sure if something bad will happen, so she has started to rely on others to tell her that everything's okay. Daily, she asks her parents multiple times for their opinion on her choices and experiences: "Do you think I studied enough for math?" "Do you think my friend's mad at me for not coming over this weekend?" "I feel dizzy—do you think I'm going to faint?" She also checks in frequently with her teachers to make sure she's interpreting their assignments and test questions correctly. When she's not with her parents, she calls and texts them repeatedly to make sure they're safe. She also frequently searches the Internet for health information, trying to gain certainty that she doesn't have some serious disease. She always feels better briefly after she gets reassurance—but then she feels she needs *more* reassurance, and she feels increasingly anxious without it.

for you to know

Recall from Activity 8 that many worriers have trouble tolerating uncertainty. They want to know for sure what's going to happen so they can be fully prepared, or they want to make sure that they've made correct decisions to prevent bad things from happening. Intolerance of uncertainty causes people to try to do things to increase certainty, like ask others for reassurance or repeatedly check for more information, as Riley does. Other examples of checking include making sure you haven't missed a text message or social media post (perhaps dozens of times a day), frequently checking the stove to make sure you didn't leave it on by accident (preventing a fire), and repeatedly going through your list of assignments to make sure you got everything done.

You may be thinking right now, *But isn't this a good thing to do? It's helpful to get other people's opinions, and double checking is conscientious!* To some extent, you're right— occasionally checking in about a tricky situation or making sure you haven't made a mistake on an important task is helpful. What we're talking about, however, is *excessive* reassurance-seeking and checking—repeatedly seeking others' opinions about even minor decisions or actions, or frequently checking for information even when you probably already know the answer. The problem with excessive reassurance-seeking and checking is that they make you think you can't trust your own judgment, or that others somehow know more than you do about things in your life. Plus, that feeling of relief you get when, for example, your mom says, "You did the right thing" or when the Internet says you probably don't have cancer makes you feel great in the short term—but then you start to rely on it to decrease your anxiety about uncertainty. You then increase your reassurance-seeking or checking more and more.

for you to do

If you do a lot of reassurance-seeking and checking, you may not even realize how much you do it. This first activity involves keeping track of your own reassurance-seeking and checking for a few days. Make sure to include at least one weekend day to see if your checking depends on the type of day. Keeping track will increase your awareness of the frequency of the behavior, which will help when you're ready to decrease how often you do it. Keep it simple—every time you catch yourself checking, place a mark on a piece of paper. Or, if you have a smartphone, download a basic "tally counter" app and press the button every time you catch yourself. Record the frequency of your behavior in the chart that follows. To download blank copies of this chart, please visit http://www.newharbinger.com/35845.

Day	Behavior	How many times did you engage in the behavior today?

Bonus exercise: Write down what you're worried will happen if you don't check or ask for reassurance. Consider using the strategies (ignoring, defusing, or challenging your worry thoughts) in Activities 9 to 11 to address these thoughts.

more to do

Now that you have a sense of how often you check or seek reassurance, practice gradually reducing these behaviors. For example, if you ask your parents an average of ten unnecessary questions a day (that is, questions you're asking only to decrease your anxiety), try to ask nine questions for two days, then eight for the next two days, and so on until you get to only one or two a day. If you're feeling brave, ask your parents, teachers, or friends to help you with this by reminding you of your goal when you're trying to cut back. Remember that it may be hard at first, but the more you practice resisting the urge to check, the easier it will get over time. Use the chart below to keep track of your progress, using Riley's example as a guide. To download blank charts, please visit http://www.newharbinger.com/35845.

Target behavior (What type of reassurance-seeking or checking are you trying to stop?): *Checking in with my mom to make sure I'm doing the right thing.*			
Day	Goal (# of times you plan to check)	Actual frequency (# of times you checked)	Any challenges?
Thursday	*8*	*7*	*I didn't think I was seeking reassurance when I texted my mom and asked where I was supposed to meet her after school, but she thought it counted as checking since she had already told me in the a.m.*

Target behavior (What type of reassurance-seeking or checking are you trying to stop?):			
Day	Goal (# of times you plan to check)	Actual frequency (# of times you checked)	Any challenges?

If it's too big of a step for you to reduce your reassurance-seeking or checking, try to delay the behavior. In other words, when you have the urge to check, see if you can wait ten minutes before doing it. Gradually increase the delay over time. You may find that if you ride out the urge to check, you don't have to do it after all.

changing your tendency to be a people pleaser 18

Nili, a high school student, loves painting, plays lacrosse, and volunteers with her church youth group. Despite being well liked by peers and adults, she worries tremendously about upsetting people or making them mad at her. Because of this fear, she constantly tries to please others, which sometimes means she doesn't get what she wants or needs. For example, when making plans with her friends, she always goes along with what others want to do instead of suggesting something she thinks would be fun to do. In art class, she pursues projects that her teacher is most excited about, which means abandoning some creative ideas she likes better. Many times Nili has been bothered by something a friend or family member has said or done, but she rarely confronts anyone. On one occasion, someone she considered to be a close friend excluded her from a planned trip to the beach. Instead of talking to her about it, Nili doubled up efforts to please her friend—inviting her to a special concert, doing the bulk of a group science project they were both working on, and texting her more often. Nili has noticed that she has trouble just enjoying time with her friends and family because she's always looking out for signs that others are displeased with her.

for you to know

Many teens are uncomfortable with confrontation, fearing they'll upset their friends, irritate teachers or coaches, or disappoint family members. *People pleasing*—always doing things to make others happy—is a common safety behavior, which (as you'll recall) is an unnecessary or excessive action designed to ward off something bad happening. Safety behaviors prevent you from seeing you're just fine without them. In this case, people pleasing keeps you from finding out what would happen if you didn't try so hard to prevent other people from getting mad at you. We're not talking about being mean or always putting your own needs above those of others, but rather finding the middle ground of asserting yourself when something is important to you. In Nili's case, she could have decided to choose an art project she was really passionate about, or she could have told her friend she was disappointed about not getting the beach invite—after all, there may have been an understandable reason why she wasn't included. Those who do a lot of people pleasing tend to overestimate the likelihood that others will be mad at or disappointed with them, but they also tend to catastrophize what will happen if someone actually does get mad at them ("They'll hate me forever!"). Sorting out disagreements is challenging but tends to make relationships stronger, not weaker, in the long run.

for you to do

This exercise will help you identify and challenge anxious thoughts associated with your people-pleasing behavior. (For more on thought challenging, see Activity 11.) To help guide you through the exercise, here's Nili's response.

Identify a situation in which you're worried about disappointing someone (or a group of people).

Deciding what to do when I hang out with my friends Christina and LaTonya. (They both have strong opinions about what we do when we hang out.)

What do you do to avoid upsetting or confronting them?

I just let them pick what we do, and if they disagree with each other, I go out of my way to help them find a compromise.

How does this "people pleasing" get in the way of your life, if at all?

When we hang out, I don't always like what they pick to do (and we never do the things I like best, like going down to the lake or the craft store).

What are you concerned will happen if you don't try to please them?

They'll be annoyed with me or just tell me "no." Maybe they won't hang out with me as much anymore.

Is there another way the situation could turn out other than the person/people getting disappointed or mad?

It's possible they might want to do what I want to do, too. Or, they might be cool with taking turns picking what we do.

If the person/people did get angry or disappointed, could you handle it? Could anything good come out of the confrontation?

This would be hard for me, but we could probably work it out. They might ask me what I want to do more often in the future.

Now it's your turn to challenge your thoughts:

Identify a situation in which you're worried about disappointing someone (or a group of people).

_____

_____

What do you do to avoid upsetting or confronting them?

_____

_____

How does this "people pleasing" get in the way of your life, if at all?

_____

_____

What are you concerned will happen if you don't try to please them?

_____

_____

_____

Is there another way the situation could turn out other than the person/people getting disappointed or mad?

_____

_____

_____

If the person/people did get angry or disappointed, could you handle it? Could anything good come out of the confrontation?

_____

_____

_____

more to do

Now that you have challenged your fears, it's time to test out what happens if you stop trying so hard to please people. First, see Nili's example to show you how to do this.

Using the situation you identified in the first exercise, write down all the ways you try to avoid upsetting or disappointing someone or a group of people. (It's okay if there are only one or two ways.)

1. *Let Christina or LaTonya decide what we're going to do.*

2. *Act excited about what they picked to do, even if I don't really want to do it.*

3. *Help them compromise if they disagree about what we do (so they're both happy).*

Now, write down what you would consider to be the "opposite" of each of the behaviors you named above. In other words, what would it look like if you challenged yourself to change the behaviors? On a scale from 0 (not at all anxiety provoking) to 10 (extremely anxiety provoking), rate how anxious you would feel if you tried each one:

Opposite behavior	Anxiety rating
1. *Suggest we do something I want to do.*	6
2. *Insist we do what I want to do.*	8
3. *Don't go out of my way to act excited about something I don't want to do.*	4
4. *Let them work out any disagreement on their own.*	3

When the situation occurs again, try to do the thing you rated the lowest on the anxiety scale. What happened?

When they disagreed about what we should do and turned to me to help them decide, I said they could figure it out without me. They did, and it ended up being no big deal. (They didn't fight all day.)

The next time you're in the situation, try another opposite behavior on your list. What happened this time?

On Saturday, I told my friends I wanted to go down to the lake. They said, "Okay, sounds good," and we stayed there most of the day. They weren't mad at me at all. (They actually seemed kind of happy I made the suggestion.)

Now it's your turn. Using the situation you identified in the first exercise, write down all the ways you try to avoid upsetting or disappointing someone or a group of people (it's okay if there are only one or two ways).

1. _____

2. _____

3. _____

4. _____

Now, write down what you would consider to be the "opposite" of each of the behaviors you named above. In other words, what would it look like if you challenged yourself to change the behaviors? On a scale from 0 (not at all anxiety provoking) to 10 (extremely anxiety provoking), rate how anxious you would feel if you tried each one:

Opposite behavior	Anxiety rating
1.	
2.	
3.	
4.	

When the situation occurs again, try to do the thing you rated the lowest on the anxiety scale. What happened?

_____

_____

_____

_____

The next time you're in the situation, try another opposite behavior on your list. What happened this time?

_____

_____

_____

_____

Keep going until you've practiced everything on your list, keeping track of what happens and how it compares with what you worried would happen. Once you have success in this situation, move on to other situations where you can practice letting go of any unhelpful people-pleasing behavior.

19 limiting overpreparation

DJ, a high school junior, has had the highest grades in his class since freshman year. Not only does he do well academically, but he also plays varsity football and has won several awards at debate tournaments. DJ has always invested a lot of time in school and extracurricular activities, but over the past year, it seems like he's been working harder and harder. Specifically, he spends long hours preparing for upcoming exams and quizzes; he's compiled elaborate files with materials he might need for debates, although he uses only a small portion of the files at actual tournaments; and he participates in every optional football practice (even though he knows the plays better than most of his teammates). Lately, he's been staying up past 1 a.m. to get everything done. His friends joke that it's like he's fallen off the face of the Earth, since they never see him. Notably, he's been making many little mistakes recently, to the point that his grades are slipping a bit. DJ tells himself, *I just have to try harder.*

for you to know

We're told from a young age that we must work hard to succeed in life. Hard work certainly does pay off, but there's a point at which piling on more and more effort doesn't produce better results (see graph below).

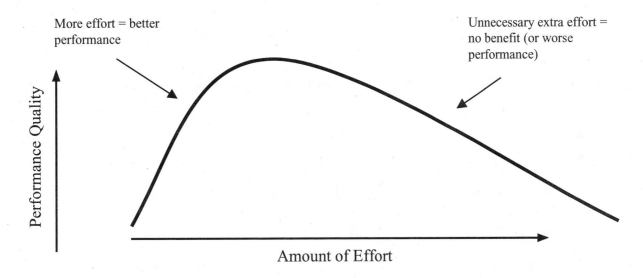

Many teens who worry about their performance in school and extracurricular activities overprepare, a needless and time-consuming safety behavior intended to prevent failure. It's tempting to put in more and more work when you're rewarded by good grades, and people praise you for being so thorough and successful. Plus, the more successful you are, the more you may worry about what you have to lose, further driving you to overprepare. However, teens who overprepare don't realize that, at a certain point, they'd perform just as well in school and extracurricular activities with less time and effort. Indeed, overpreparing steals time and energy that could be spent elsewhere. In DJ's case, he spent less time hanging out with his friends because he was consumed by his work. He also became so exhausted that his performance suffered. He didn't realize that he needed more rest and downtime to have the mental and physical energy necessary to perform at his best.

for you to do

This exercise will help you identify and ignore the worry thoughts you associate with overpreparing. (See Activity 9, Ignoring Unhelpful Thoughts, for more details.)

What do you tend to overprepare for?

_____

What are you worried will happen if you cut back on the amount of time or effort you put into this task?

_____

_____

Are your worries like any of these types of junk mail thinking? Check if yes.

- ☐ All-or-nothing thinking (making extreme judgments: "I'm either a success or a failure, and there's nothing in between")

- ☐ Catastrophizing (believing the worst will happen: "I'm going to fail, and that would be so horrible")

- ☐ Mind reading (thinking you know what others are thinking: "My teacher will think I'm not trying hard enough")

- ☐ Overresponsibility (believing it's all on you to prevent bad things from happening: "If I do poorly, it will be all my fault for not trying harder")

- ☐ Intolerance of uncertainty (believing you must know what will happen in the future: "If I keep working, I can be *sure* that I won't do badly")

Based on what you checked off, practice labeling these junk mail thoughts as they occur—for example, "That's my all-or-nothing thinking bothering me again." In DJ's case, when he told himself that he just had to try harder, he could have countered by saying, "There I go again with the overresponsibility."

more to do

Many overpreparers predict that they'll perform less well if they reduce the amount of time they spend on their activities. This exercise will test that hypothesis, while helping you gradually cut back on the amount of time you spend preparing.

The exercise will focus on overpreparing for academic work, like studying too long for tests, spending excessive amounts of time on writing assignments, or rehearsing an oral presentation more times than necessary. Over the next few weeks, set a goal to gradually reduce the amount of time you spend on these academic activities. For example, if you normally spend four hours preparing for a test, try to cut back to three hours the first week, then two hours the following week, and so on until you reach the amount of time that's appropriate given the complexity of the work. If you have trouble figuring out what's "an appropriate amount of time," it's okay to consult with teachers, counselors, or parents (so long as you don't repeatedly ask them for reassurance that you're working hard enough!).

Test out your prediction that you will do less well by cutting back on your overpreparing, using the chart below. See the top line for an example from DJ's case. To download blank copies of the chart, please visit http://www.newharbinger.com /35845.

Date	Subject/type of assignment	Time spent on assignment	Predicted grade	Actual grade
Example: *May 10*	*History test*	*2.25 hours (normally would spend 3–4 hours)*	*C+*	*A–*

How did your actual grades compare with your predicted grades?

_____

_____

Did your grades drop significantly from when you overprepared?

_____

conquering distraction and procrastination 20

Ethan, a high school senior, has been told many times by his parents and teachers to get started on long projects a week or two before they're actually due. He tends to not take this advice because he finds writing projects very challenging, and he has trouble doing things that make him anxious if he doesn't absolutely *have* to do them. When Ethan has deadlines approaching, his anxiety is triggered, and he does all he can to avoid thinking of the work he has to do. He distracts himself by playing hours of video games and watching shows online, which gives him temporary relief from his anxiety. This relief lasts only until the next time he thinks about starting his work, with his anxiety rising steadily as the deadlines get closer. Recently, his procrastination has gotten to the point that he has asked his teachers for extra time to complete his work.

for you to know

In some situations, distraction can be a helpful coping strategy. When you're in a stressful situation that's outside of your control—like waiting to hear if you've been accepted to a school you want to go to, or being stuck in an airport because your flight is delayed indefinitely—engaging in a distracting activity can help keep you from thinking about the situation nonstop. In addition, when you're very distressed about something to the point that you can't think logically, short periods of distraction can help reduce the intensity of your distress until you're able to use more effective coping skills, like problem solving (see Activity 21). On the other hand, when you use distraction with the sole purpose of avoiding anxious thoughts and feelings, it actually increases your anxiety over time, similar to Ethan's experience—you're basically sending yourself the message that the situation you're avoiding is a big threat.

Procrastination is when you put off tasks you don't want to do, often because they make you feel anxious or uncomfortable, or they involve a lot of hard work. *Distraction* is one method of procrastination in which you do something that will take your mind off of the task you're avoiding. For example, imagine you want to find a summer job, but you have to call possible employers to ask if they're hiring. You're anxious about making the phone calls (*What if they say no and hang up on me? What if they think my question is dumb?*), so you decide to play a game on your phone instead of calling. Using distraction in this way is like saying to yourself, *This task is so awful that I can't handle it,* which then increases your anxiety the next time you consider making those calls. Higher anxiety then increases the chances that (a) you continue to put it off until you *must* do it (often with little time and much stress, likely diminishing the quality of your work), or (b) it never gets done (resulting in poorer grades or lost opportunities).

Breaking the cycle of procrastination is challenging, especially if you think you have to do everything you're avoiding all at once. Consider Ethan's cycle of procrastination (opposite). Notice that it's another form of the worry cycle (see Activity 2).

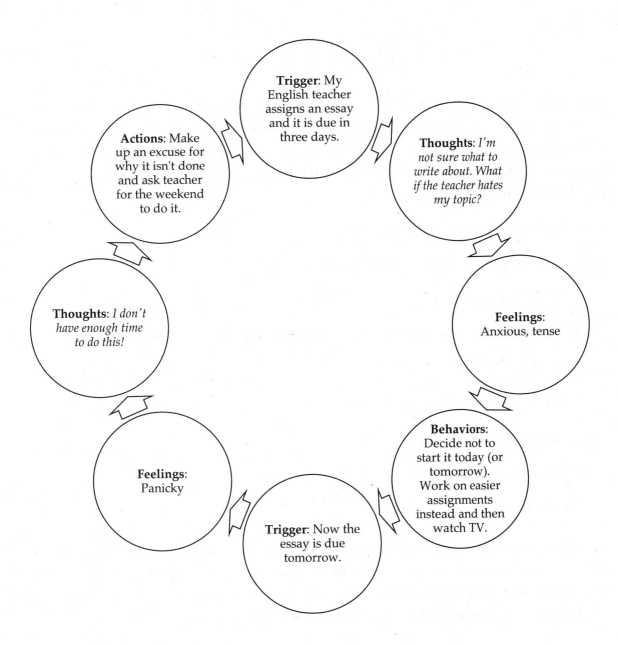

To break the cycle of procrastination (or at least slow it down), Ethan could make changes at several different points along the way. For example, he could try to challenge his initial anxious thoughts using thought-challenging strategies in Activity 11: *I've always been able to come up with something to write about, even if it isn't perfect.* He could also change his initial avoidance by gradually facing the task (see Activity 14). For instance, he could have tried to do a little bit of the essay each day so that it wasn't so overwhelming.

for you to do

Below is a list of common distractions that teens use when they're avoiding something that makes them feel anxious. Remember that these are normal activities that many people enjoy, but they turn into unhelpful distractions when used, sometimes for hours on end, to avoid tasks or situations that elicit anxiety. Put a check by the unhelpful distractions you use most.

☐ Watching TV or streaming videos

☐ Checking social media or text messages

☐ Browsing the Internet

☐ Chatting with friends (texting, talking on the phone, or video chatting)

☐ Eating

☐ Playing video or computer games

☐ Napping

☐ Reading a magazine or book

☐ Other: _____

Now that you've identified the distractions that get in your way, try to reduce your use of distraction with the strategies that follow. After trying each strategy for a few days, write down how well it worked for you and if you encountered any challenges. Then, regularly use the strategy or strategies that were most effective.

1.   Set a time limit on how long you'll engage in the distraction. Use a timer and stop when it goes off. Gradually reduce the amount of time you spend using the distraction (for example, five minutes less each day).

How well did this strategy work for you? _____

Did you have any challenges in using the strategy? _____

_____

2.   For social media and other websites, use one of the many commercially available apps designed to temporarily block your access to the websites on your computer or other devices. Similar to #1 (above), you can decide how long you want to block the website. The beauty of this strategy, though, is that it eliminates the temptation to give in before the time is up.

How well did this strategy work for you? _____

Did you have any challenges in using the strategy? _____

_____

3.   Use the activity as a reward instead of a distraction. (After all, these activities are definitely fun and relaxing when used appropriately.) Decide to engage in an avoided activity for a certain amount of time (for example, an hour), and then when the time is up, do the activity you would normally have used as a distraction. For example, after an hour of writing an essay, watch thirty minutes of TV.

How well did this strategy work for you? _____

Did you have any challenges in using the strategy? _____

_____

more to do

Relying less on distracting activities is one step toward halting the procrastination cycle. The next step is to make anxiety-provoking tasks more manageable and therefore less overwhelming.

First, try the *five-minute rule*: before you avoid doing the task that's making you anxious, try doing it for five minutes (set a timer if that helps you). If at the end of the five minutes you decide you don't want to keep doing it, then stop and try again later. On the other hand, if you find that you can continue beyond the five minutes, then by all means, keep going! The five-minute rule targets one of the hardest parts of a tough task: getting started.

Second, break the task into smaller, more manageable pieces. As we discussed above, this is a strategy that could be helpful to Ethan: dividing the number of pages of his essay into three, and writing that number of pages each day until the essay is due. Similarly, in our example of putting off calls to find a summer job, rather than making all the calls in one day, you could decide to make one call per day. Alternatively, when you have an overwhelming task, you can list all the steps you need to take to reach the final goal and then do one or two of the steps at a time. Here's how to do this, using Ethan's situation as a guide.

Step 1. Describe the lengthy or overwhelming task you need to complete.

My English essay

Step 2. List all the subtasks you need to do to finish.

   a. *Select a topic.*

   b. *Create a thesis statement.*

   c. *Outline the essay.*

   d. *Write a rough draft.*

   e. *Write a final draft.*

Step 3. Determine how many days you have before it's due. If there's no due date, consider the ideal time frame for completing the task.

I have three days.

Step 4. Assign one or two subtasks to each day you have available to work before the project is due. Be realistic—assume each subtask will take longer than you expect, so give yourself as much time as possible to complete each one.

Day 1: Select my topic, write my thesis statement, and start the outline.

Day 2: Finish the outline, write the rough draft.

Day 3: Write the final draft.

Now it's your turn:

Step 1. Describe the lengthy or overwhelming task you need to complete.

_____

_____

Step 2. List all the subtasks you need to do to finish. If you get stuck breaking tasks into smaller steps, remember that you can get suggestions from your support network (that is, teachers, parents, tutor, and/or guidance counselor).

a. _____

b. _____

c. _____

d. _____

e. _____

Step 3. Determine how many days you have before it's due. If there's no due date, consider the ideal time frame for completing the task.

_____

Step 4. Assign one or two subtasks to each day you have available to work before the project is due. Be realistic—assume each subtask will take longer than you expect, so give yourself as much time as possible to complete each one.

Day   *Subtask(s) to complete*

_____   _____

_____   _____

_____   _____

_____   _____

_____   _____

Learning to prioritize and schedule are important skills that will help you deal more effectively with distraction and procrastination. For more help in learning these skills, please see online Activity 29 (Prioritizing and Scheduling Tasks). Because distraction and procrastination can also play a role in test anxiety, please see online Activity 30 (Tackling Test Anxiety) for more helpful information and exercises. Both activities can be found at http://www.newharbinger.com/35845.

for you to know

As we've discussed, you (and other worried teens) are pretty good at imagining all possible worst-case scenarios. At the same time, you may underestimate your ability to handle tough situations, which feeds the worry cycle: believing you won't know what to do → increases your worry/anxiety → strengthens your belief that you can't handle the situation. You may also doubt your decisions, or have trouble making decisions in the first place, in the face of overwhelming options. You may prefer to have someone else solve the problem for you or to avoid the problem altogether.

This activity will provide a framework that will help you when you're faced with a tough problem, particularly when there's no clear "right" or "wrong" way to handle it. Consider Jen, a fifteen-year-old girl who tends to worry about her friendships (specifically, that her friends will get mad at her and exclude her). She spends the most time with two different friend groups—her school friends and her friends from her dance studio. One of her good friends from school, Marisa, invites Jen to her upcoming "Sweet Sixteen" birthday party. Later that day, one of her dance friends, Shana, tells her that she's also having a "Sweet Sixteen" birthday party—the same exact day and time as Marisa's. Jen cares very much for both friends and thinks she would have the same amount of fun at either party. But she's worried that if she misses one of the parties, that friend will be hurt and angry. She tells her mom she doesn't know what to do.

Her mom teaches her a helpful way to solve problems. You can use this same approach when you have a problem that bothers you. It involves answering questions that guide you toward the best solution to the problem. See the questions (and Jen's answers) below.

What exactly is the problem?

Two of my good friends are having birthday parties on the same day, at the same time, and I want to go to both of them.

What are all of the possible solutions to the problem? Feel free to brainstorm and write down whatever comes to mind, even if it seems silly or far-fetched.

a. *Go to Shana's party, but don't go to Marisa's.*

b. *Go to Marisa's party, but don't go to Shana's.*

c. *Try to go to a part of each party.*

d. *Don't go to either party (make up an excuse, like I'll be away that weekend).*

What are the pros/cons of each of the solutions you've generated?

a./b. **Pros:** *I won't have to find two rides, I won't have to leave if I'm having fun, and one of my friends will be really happy I'm there the whole time.*

  Cons: *I'll miss the other friend's party (and she might be sad or mad about that).*

c. **Pros:** *I'll make both friends happy, I'll be happy to share in both of my friends' special days, and it might be more fun to be at part of each party.*

  Cons: *I'll have to find two rides; I might miss a part of each party that I would have enjoyed.*

d. **Pros:** *No one has to feel hurt that I'm choosing one friend over the other; I get relief from not having to decide.*

  Cons: *I would feel bad lying—plus, I'd miss the chance to enjoy myself with my friends.*

Based on the pros/cons, what's the best solution or combination of solutions?

The best solution is to go to the beginning of Marisa's party and the end of Shana's (since Shana's party is only twenty minutes from Marisa's, it's doable).

for you to do

Think of a problem you're facing (or one that you recently faced). Some common problems include having several big assignments or exams all due on the same day; being caught in the middle of a disagreement between friends or family members; not being able to complete a task by its due date; or breaking/damaging something important to you or someone else. Once you've identified a problem, use these questions to guide you toward a solution.

What exactly is the problem?

_____

What are all of the possible solutions to the problem? Feel free to brainstorm and write down whatever comes to mind, even if it seems silly or far-fetched.

a. _____

b. _____

c. _____

d. _____

e. _____

Look at your solutions above. What are the pros/cons of each? To download blank copies of this chart, please visit http://www.newharbinger.com/35845.

Solution	Pros	Cons
a.		
b.		
c.		
d.		
e.		

Based on the pros/cons, what's the best solution or combination of solutions?

_____

_____

more to do

Sometimes executing a solution is the most challenging part of problem solving. Look at the solution you've identified as the best option in the first exercise. Use the steps below to figure out what you need to do to make the solution happen, and then generate one or two backup plans in case your initial plan doesn't work out. See Jen's action plan as an example.

How will you carry out the solution you've selected?

I'll ask my mom and dad if one of them can drive me to both parties.

What could go wrong with this plan? If that happens, what else can you do?

My parents might be busy or can only take me to one (not both) of the parties. If that happens, I'll ask my Aunt Allison if she can take me.

What could go wrong with the backup plan? If that happens, what else can you do?

It's possible my parents and aunt will all be busy. If that happens, I'll ask an older friend to drive me to Marisa's party, and then my friend Anna (who is going to Shana's party) can likely take me to and from the second party.

Now it's your turn:

How will you carry out the solution you've selected?

_____

_____

What could go wrong with this plan? If that happens, what else can you do?

_____

_____

_____

_____

What could go wrong with the backup plan? If that happens, what else can you do?

_____

_____

_____

_____

managing social media 22

Sophie spends countless hours on her phone or computer, especially on weekends. The fifteen-year-old girl finds it easiest to communicate with her friends via text and various social media, but she also loves to see other people's pictures and posts about what they're doing. The problem is that she persistently worries that people (including people she doesn't even know) will think her own pics and posts are kind of dumb, so she can't stop checking the number of "likes" and comments she gets after she has posted something. After an hour, if a post isn't getting as much approval as her prior posts (or her friends' posts), she deletes it, assuming that people are criticizing it. Sophie also scrutinizes what others post. If she sees a group of acquaintances having fun together, she thinks, *Everyone has more friends than I do,* or *I don't get to go out as much as other people do.* After spending a lot of time on social media, she tends to feel discouraged and worried about where she stands with her peers.

for you to know

Don't be alarmed—this activity is not about swearing off social media forever. In fact, social media has many benefits. It gives you the opportunity to stay in close contact with your friends and family, including people you don't get to see very often, and it allows you to get to know people better, which might help you figure out with whom you want to spend more time in real life. Social media also keeps you in the loop about activities you might want to join in on. In addition, it can be a welcome distraction when you're bored (though, as we discussed in Activity 20, beware of social media as an unhelpful procrastination method).

For all its perks, social media can also be a source of stress, whether you're a worrier or not. Seeing pictures of other people's adventures can create fear of missing out and reinforce all-or-nothing thinking that everyone else lives a fabulous life while you're stuck at home. After all, most people don't post pictures of themselves watching TV alone in their pajamas.

There's also a lot of ambiguity on social media. Just like in real life, you can't know for sure what others are thinking—but because interactions online tend to be brief, and you don't know whether someone has seen your post or not, social media can exacerbate your mind reading (believing that others are judging you negatively). For example, if someone doesn't wish you a happy birthday, does it mean he doesn't like you, or was he just not on social media that day? Or maybe he doesn't wish anyone a happy birthday—who knows? Mind reading can also operate in reverse: you might be very quick to respond to other people's posts because you don't want them to think you don't like them!

Another downside to social media is that it reinforces the need for external validation—in other words, it causes you to believe that social approval is a measure of your worth as a person. That's why Sophie cares how many likes and comments she gets on her posts. When she gets a lot of approval, she feels more confident that she's a likable (and therefore worthwhile) person. That process can undermine other sources of self-esteem, such as being very special to a few close friends or devoting yourself to activities that may not be the most popular, but are things you enjoy or are good at.

Unfortunately, social media can also provide a platform for purposely bringing other people down because of a fight or misunderstanding. For example, one teen might engage in public shaming by posting, "I thought I knew who my good friends were, but guess I was wrong," while tagging the offending person in the post to make a statement. In some cases, this kind of mean behavior crosses the line into *cyberbullying* (that is, repeatedly harassing someone online or via text messages). Dealing with cyberbullying is beyond the scope of this activity, but if you suspect you or someone you know is a victim, talk to your parents or guidance counselor to make a plan for dealing with this kind of toxic behavior.

This activity will help you stay focused on the fun and beneficial aspects of social media. It will also help you cut back on unhelpful social media practices and get some space from it when it becomes more stressful than rewarding.

for you to do

Recall that Activity 19 focused on overpreparing for school and extracurricular activities. Similarly, many worried teens report that they feel compelled to manage their social media profiles like it's their job. They agonize over which pictures to post versus delete, and they read over any written post or comment multiple times to make sure it sounds good enough. Clearly, second-guessing takes up a lot of time and undermines your trust that people like you as you are. Try this exercise to challenge your efforts to control what people think of you.

Do you tend to micromanage your social media profiles and posts? If so, describe your behavior(s):

_____

_____

_____

_____

What do you predict will happen if you stop excessively managing your profiles and posts?

_____

_____

_____

_____

Circle one or two ways that you'd be willing to challenge your tendency to micromanage social media:

a. Post a comment after reviewing it just once. If you tend to review it four or five times, then gradually cut back until you get to one.

b. Pick which picture to post within one minute (versus many minutes of internal debate).

c. Allow a friend to pick which picture you post.

d. Purposely post a picture that is kind of silly or even a little unflattering.

e. Other challenge: _____

For the next week, put the challenge you selected into action. Did your prediction come true? Did you notice any changes in the number of likes or comments you usually get on posts?

_____

_____

If your negative prediction did come true, how bad was it really? Were you able to cope with what happened?

_____

_____

For her part, Sophie worried that if her photos didn't get many likes or comments, then people would start acting more distant toward her at school (*Maybe they're thinking about me differently now*). Her challenge was to keep the less popular photos posted on her social media pages. She did this for a week and observed that friends and classmates treated her no differently than they did before.

more to do

Social media keeps you hooked by delivering instant feelings of reward and satisfaction the moment you get a favorable response or see that someone has sent you a message. Just like someone pulling a lever on a casino slot machine in hopes of getting a payout, you feel compelled to keep checking social media for new likes and interesting posts. There are times, though, that you deserve a break from the whole social media environment. A break might be especially welcome if you're concerned about the amount of time social media takes up, when it distracts you from taking part in more important activities (ahem: homework), when you just can't stop checking your phone or computer even when you want to, or when you're feeling stressed by what other people post.

The ideal would be to go a whole day without checking social media and observing what effect this has on your thoughts and feelings. If that's too challenging right now, try a shorter time-out. For instance, if you normally check multiple times an hour, then try to take a one-hour break from social media. If you can easily go an hour without checking but a full day is too challenging, try a four-hour break. To help you stick with the break, try these approaches:

- Temporarily delete the social media apps from your phone (you can reinstall them later).

- Use commercially available apps that block your use of whatever website you choose for the duration of time you decide upon.

- Put your phone and/or computer out of your sight. If you're willing, ask a family member or friend to hold on to your devices for the length of the break.

- Do something that's incompatible with using social media. For example, go for a walk with your dog, play a game with a family member, or read a book or magazine.

As you gain success with taking a break from social media, gradually increase the duration of the break until you can take an occasional full day off. You don't have to take a break every day if you don't want to, but taking time away from social media when it isn't fun will give you the space you need to let go of unhelpful thoughts and feelings that social media can sometimes trigger.

Section Five

Mind-Body Strategies
to Reduce Worry

23 fitting exercise into your life

for you to know

I have no doubt that many adults in your life have told you to get outside and exercise. At the risk of sounding like your parents, it's true that regular physical exercise is associated with a whole range of good outcomes: improved sleep, reduced stress and muscle tension, better mood, and less anxiety. In fact, recent research has shown that cardiovascular exercise and resistance training can be helpful for those with anxiety and mood problems (Asmundson et al. 2013; Otto and Smits 2011). All the same, life in middle and high school is demanding—between school, homework, extracurricular and social activities, after-school jobs or volunteer work, and time with your family, it's no wonder you may have a hard time fitting exercise into your schedule if you aren't part of a sports team. Further, some teens hate to exercise because it can be uncomfortable, boring, or both. Thus, the challenge is to find the time and motivation to exercise enough that you reap its mental and physical benefits.

Mia, an eighth grader, has struggled to exercise. She jokes that she's the opposite of a natural athlete, and she's far more likely to be found in the library or watching videos with her friends than on an athletic field or in the gym. At the same time, she's noticed how tired and rundown she often feels, even when she gets enough sleep. She also feels tense and jittery, especially when she's worried about something. Her mom told her (again) that getting some exercise might help her to feel less stressed. They brainstormed about different options that might be at least somewhat appealing to Mia, and she decided she would be most likely to try yoga since her best friend does it, and there are multiple places in town that offer yoga at a student discount. She and her mom looked up classes and put them in the calendar for the next couple of weeks.

for you to do

Below is a list of different types of physical exercise. Examine the list and check off every activity that you'd be willing to try (or do more often), taking into consideration your level of interest, convenience (can you easily engage in the activity?), affordability (some sports involve a lot of equipment), and social aspects (do you prefer solo activities or those that involve other people?).

☐ Basketball (or shooting hoops)	☐ Skateboarding
☐ Biking	☐ Skiing
☐ Cardio machines at the gym	☐ Soccer
☐ Dancing	☐ Strength training
☐ Geocaching	☐ Swimming
☐ Hiking	☐ Throwing around a ball or Frisbee
☐ Ice skating	☐ Volleyball
☐ Lifting weights	☐ Walking
☐ Martial arts	☐ Yard work
☐ Paintball	☐ Yoga
☐ Rowing or kayaking	☐ _____
☐ Running or jogging	☐ _____

Look at the types of fitness activities you checked off: which activity or activities are you *most* likely to do? Now that you have selected at least one activity, look at your schedule for the next week. Identify two or three times when you could take part in the activity/activities, and then block out those times in your schedule to make sure you don't do something else instead. (See online Activity 29 for more scheduling strategies.) If you don't have a schedule or calendar, think of times when you tend to be free. For example, if you usually have two hours after school before you start homework, could you devote two or three afternoons a week to the activity?

more to do

Having thought about the type of exercise that would work best for you and when to do it, let's look at the connection between exercise and your worry and mood. Keep an exercise and mood log for the next three to four weeks, using the chart below. (To download extra charts, please visit http://www.newharbinger.com/35845.) Rate your worry level on a scale from 0 (not at all worried) to 10 (extremely worried); similarly, rate how sad or down you felt that day on a scale from 0 (not at all sad/down) to 10 (extremely sad/down). After a few weeks, what do you notice about your worry and mood levels on the days you exercise versus the days you don't?

Date	Did you exercise today? If so, what did you do?	How long?	How worried were you today? (0–10)	How sad or down were you today? (0–10)

creating better sleep habits 24

for you to know

In adolescence, sleep patterns skew toward going to bed later (and getting up later in the morning), with most teens needing eight to ten hours of sleep per night to feel well rested (National Sleep Foundation Sleep and Teens Task Force 2000). However, start times for school tend to be very early, which makes it pretty hard to go to bed late and still get sufficient sleep. For example, if you usually go to bed at 11 p.m. and wake up at 5:30 a.m. for school, you're only getting six and a half hours of sleep a night—this means you're short at least seven and a half hours of sleep by Friday morning. No wonder you're tempted to sleep until noon on Saturday—though, as you'll see below, that isn't really the best solution to the whole sleep deprivation problem.

As a worrier, you may have even more trouble getting the sleep you need because of *insomnia* (that is, difficulty falling or staying asleep). Since bedtime is free from distraction, worry thoughts may swoop in and occupy your mental space. These worries can trigger physical feelings of anxiety (for example, heart beating faster, muscle tension), which keep you awake even longer.

Worry combined with poor sleep habits is a recipe for chronic sleep deprivation—and naturally, sleep deprivation increases your vulnerability to further stress and anxiety. This vicious cycle can be targeted using a range of strategies. Other activities in this workbook will help you manage your worry thoughts (see Section Three: Dealing with Worry Thoughts), get adequate exercise (Activity 23), and learn to relax your body (Activity 25), all of which are important for sleep. This activity will help you identify and change unhelpful sleep habits that contribute to the cycle of sleepiness.

Jesse is a tenth grader who is sometimes so tired he nods off in his afternoon classes. He hates when he has trouble paying attention because then he worries even more that he doesn't understand what's going on in class, so he has a flavored coffee drink most afternoons. He doesn't get home from swim practice until 5 p.m., and then he takes a quick break before dinner, which means he doesn't start his homework until dinner is done (usually around 6:15). He has every intention of exclusively doing his homework for the next two hours, but inevitably, he gets interrupted by messages from friends, his sister coming into the room to chat, and quick breaks to check social media. The next thing he knows, it's 10 p.m. and he still has work to do. Sometimes he can finish quickly and get to bed before 11, but some nights he's not in bed until midnight. After concentrating so hard on his work, it takes him another half hour to slow down his thoughts and relax his body. When the alarm goes off at 5:45 the next morning, he feels like he could sleep forever—but instead, it's time to start another day.

for you to do

This exercise will help you identify poor sleep habits that may contribute to difficulty falling or staying asleep, or not getting enough sleep. Place a check next to each behavior that's typical of you (that is, occurs more than two to three days a week).

Category 1: Inconsistent Sleep Schedule

☐ The time I go to bed and get up in the morning varies a lot from day to day.

☐ On the weekends, I sleep in a lot (that is, stay in bed three or more hours later than my weekday wake-up time).

☐ I take long naps.

Note: When you frequently change your sleep and wake times, your body has trouble figuring out when it should get tired and when it should be alert. If you have trouble getting adequate sleep, you might be tempted to take long naps or sleep in for hours on the weekends, but this just further disrupts your natural sleep rhythms. To address this set of problems, see the strategies in "More to Do" (on page 135).

Category 2: Psychoactive Substances

☐ I drink coffee or soda in the afternoon or evening.

☐ I eat chocolate after dinner.

☐ I drink alcohol at parties with my friends.

Note: Caffeine is a stimulant, and when consumed after noon, it may still be in your system at bedtime, keeping you awake; chocolate contains caffeine and should be limited before bed. Alcohol may make you feel sleepy at first, but it disrupts your sleep patterns, leading to restless sleep.

Category 3: Screen Time and Using Bed for Nonsleep Activities

☐ I use my bed for studying or watching TV/videos.

☐ I use my phone or computer right up until I go to bed.

☐ I study right before bedtime.

Note: When you engage in mentally stimulating activities right up until bedtime, you may need some time to switch gears and feel relaxed (something Jesse experienced). Try to stop studying, chatting with friends, watching TV, and using your phone or computer at least thirty minutes before bedtime.

If you use your bed for activities other than sleeping, you come to associate bed with being awake—not so helpful when you need some rest. Find a different place for studying and screen time.

Finally, there's evidence that the backlight on your phone and computer tricks your brain into staying awake because it suppresses melatonin, a hormone responsible for regulating sleep/wake cycles (Cajochen et al. 2011). Instead of scrolling through your phone as you're trying to fall asleep, try to listen to some relaxing music or read a magazine.

Category 4: Suboptimal Sleep Environment

☐ My room tends to be warm.

☐ I keep the bedside lamp on in my room.

Note: It is hard to sleep when you're physically uncomfortable, so keep your bedroom on the cooler side if at all possible. Keeping a lamp on in your room may signal your brain to stay awake. A completely dark room is best for sleep, but if you must have a light, use a small nightlight plugged in away from your bed.

more to do

This exercise will help you develop a more consistent sleep schedule. To start, keep a "sleep log" every day for a week. To download a blank sleep log, please visit http://www.newharbinger.com/35845.

Day	When did you wake up this morning?	Did you take any naps today? If so, how long?	When did you get into bed with the intention of sleeping?	How long did it take you to fall asleep?

Take a look at your data. If you see a lot of variation, try these strategies:

Select an optimal bedtime. Consider when you have to wake up most mornings and then subtract at least eight hours from this time to determine your bedtime. For Jesse, since he had to get up at 5:45 a.m., his optimal bedtime was 9:45 p.m. If you've been going to bed a lot later than your optimal bedtime (like Jesse), gradually push your bedtime back. For example, Jesse went to bed at 11 p.m. for the first three days, then he pushed his bedtime to 10:30 p.m. for the next few days, and so on until he consistently went to bed at 9:45. To remind you it's time to start getting ready for bed, set an alarm to go off fifteen to twenty minutes before bedtime. Do your best to stick to this time (plus or minus thirty minutes) most days of the week.

If you think your calculated bedtime sounds too early for you, think about whether you can shave any time off of your morning routine so you can get up a little later (and thus go to bed a little later).

Have a consistent wake-up time. As tempting as it may be to sleep until noon on Saturday and Sunday mornings, this behavior makes it very challenging to go to sleep Sunday night. Challenge yourself to get up by 9:00 a.m. on the weekends during the school year.

Limit napping. Some people find a regular thirty- to forty-five-minute afternoon nap refreshes them for the rest of the day. Longer naps tend to lead to feelings of sluggishness, and they interfere with being able to stick to a regular bedtime and wake-up time. If you have trouble sleeping at night, it may be best to avoid napping to increase the likelihood that you'll feel tired at your optimal bedtime.

As you put these changes into action, continue to keep your sleep log. After a week or two, see if you notice more regularity in your sleep schedule. Also notice if it takes less time to fall asleep after getting into bed. If you continue to struggle with your sleep despite your best efforts to create better sleep habits, consider making an appointment with your doctor, who will determine if more evaluation and intervention are needed.

for you to know

Progressive muscle relaxation (PMR) is a helpful relaxation exercise for people who experience a lot of muscle tension (often caused by unconsciously tightening muscles when stressed), or who have difficulty falling asleep at night. Relaxation techniques can also be useful for lowering overall physical symptoms of anxiety or stress, such as feelings of restlessness or hyperreactivity to stimuli like loud noises. PMR works to lower your body's typical level of stress and to relieve muscle tension. PMR and other relaxation techniques are generally *not* helpful once you're highly anxious since your body is already too far into "panic mode" and just needs some time to calm itself down (which it will do eventually). Indeed, when you're panicking, trying to take deep breaths or relax your body can be an exercise in frustration—if it doesn't work, it just increases your fear that you won't stop feeling panicky. PMR and other relaxation strategies should be practiced *proactively*—that is, when you aren't feeling highly anxious—with the goal of gradually reducing physical feelings of stress over time.

For example, Kayla tends to feel jittery or "on edge" during the school year when she's most worried about social and academic stressors. At times, she gets so worried about things that could go wrong that her heart beats fast, her thoughts race, and she has trouble catching her breath. Her parents tell her to just slow down and take a deep breath during these moments, but she finds this to be nearly impossible to do once she's already worked up and upset. Her counselor suggests that it might be more useful to practice taking slow deep breaths five minutes a day when she's not already feeling panicky. Kayla decides to devote five minutes to deep breathing every day when she gets home from school, which has led to her feeling calmer later in the evening as she completes homework.

PMR is also best practiced once a day during periods of relative calm. PMR involves gradually tightening and relaxing all of the muscle groups in your body from head to toe. The exercise is kind of like a mini-massage as it slowly releases muscle tension. Some teens find it easier to do a relaxation exercise that focuses on a concrete action (tightening and releasing the muscles), compared with certain types of meditation that involve sitting with your thoughts and feelings.

for you to do

To understand how PMR works to relax your body, take a moment to tightly squeeze your fist, as if you were tightly gripping an object. Hold the grip for thirty seconds, then slowly unfold your hand. What do you notice? Most likely, you're experiencing a warm, tingly feeling spreading through your hand. Compared with the tension in your hand a moment ago, this may be a welcome and relaxing sensation. Now, imagine your whole body feeling just as relaxed—that's the goal of PMR!

The PMR exercise you will learn below includes some slow deep breathing in between tightening and relaxing muscle groups. To prepare for the exercise, practice your deep-breathing skills. First, sit in a comfortable chair with your feet flat on the floor. Next, place a hand on the lower part of your stomach, also known as your diaphragm, and your other hand on your upper chest—this will serve as a check to be sure you're breathing from your belly (deeper, more relaxing breaths) and not from your chest (shallower breaths). If you're having difficulty breathing from your belly, try lying on your back with a paperback book on your stomach—as you breathe in, the book should rise, and as you breathe out, the book should lower.

Take a breath from your belly—as you inhale, count "one," and as you exhale, count "two." Repeat—one, two, one, two (and so on for approximately five minutes). Breathe slowly, because breathing rapidly, even from your belly, can cause you to feel light-headed. It should take a few seconds to inhale and five to ten seconds to exhale. Once you've mastered slow deep breathing, move on to the PMR exercise.

more to do

As you learn PMR, practice when you're not already experiencing high levels of anxiety or stress, and make sure you have ten to fifteen minutes of uninterrupted time available. It's hard to learn a new skill if you're jittery, distracted, and/or interrupted. Many teens practice before bedtime or just after they get home from school. Once you've selected a good practice time, follow the instructions below. Assuming you don't want to read this book as you're trying to relax your body, consider recording yourself (or someone else) reading the instructions and listen to the recording as you do the exercise. Another option is to search online for one of many prerecorded PMR scripts (keeping in mind that these exercises may be more or less detailed or lengthy than the one included here). Otherwise, you might consider learning the important aspects of the script and running yourself through the exercise from memory.

To prepare for PMR, if you're wearing anything uncomfortable, loosen it or take it off. Find a comfortable chair. You can also practice PMR while lying down—just keep in mind that you might fall asleep while doing this. That may be a good thing if your goal is to fall asleep more easily, but if you're still learning the exercise and tend to fall asleep in the middle of it, move to a seated position.

Practice the PMR exercise daily for the first week, and then three to four times per week thereafter (or as needed). Consider setting a reminder on your phone or computer (or other device) so you won't forget to practice.

> *Sit with your feet on the floor, legs uncrossed. Close your eyes if you're comfortable doing so. Take a deep breath in, and say* relax *to yourself as you exhale. First, you'll tighten and relax the muscles in your forehead and face. Scrunch your eyes, nose, and lips, as if you have just bitten into something sour. Hold this tight feeling for ten seconds—and then relax the muscles in your face. Notice the difference between the tense feeling in your face and the relaxed feeling. Sit with this feeling for a few moments. Take a deep breath in, and say* relax *to yourself as you exhale.*

Next, focus on the muscles in your neck. Bring your chin toward your chest until they touch, and hold this position for ten seconds. Notice the tension in the back of your neck. Slowly raise your chin, paying attention to the relaxed feeling in your neck. After ten seconds, take a deep breath in and then exhale (relax). Now, raise your shoulders as high as they will go, as if you're trying to touch your ears. Hold the tension in your shoulders for ten seconds—and then slowly lower your shoulders. For the next ten seconds, pay attention to the warm, relaxed feeling in your shoulders and neck. Breathe deeply and slowly.

Next, you'll focus on the muscles in your chest. Take a really deep breath and hold it for ten seconds, noticing the tension in your chest. Exhale and sit with the feeling of relaxation in your chest muscles for a few moments. Now, direct your attention to the muscles in your arms and hands. Make tight fists with your hands and raise your arms off your lap (kind of like Superman holds his arms while flying). Hold the tension in your arms and hands for ten seconds—and then slowly bring your arms down and unfold your hands. Notice the warm and tingly sensations in your muscles for the next few moments. Take a deep breath, and exhale (relax).

You will tense and relax your abdominal muscles next. Tighten your abs, pulling them back toward your spine and holding the tension for ten seconds. Release the muscles in your abs, noticing the difference between the tight feeling and the relaxed feeling in your stomach. Hang out with this relaxed feeling for ten seconds. Inhale, then slowly exhale (relax). Next, squeeze the muscles in your thighs and glutes (pressing your thighs together). Hold this for ten seconds and then release the muscles. Feel the release of tension in your thighs and bottom as you sink deeper into your chair. Take a deep breath in, and slowly exhale (relax).

Next, focus on the muscles in your legs. Raise your legs off the ground while flexing your feet (pointing your toes upward). Hold this position for ten seconds, paying attention to the tense feeling in your legs. Slowly lower your feet to the ground. Appreciate the warm and relaxed sensation for the next few moments. Take a deep breath, reminding yourself to relax *as you exhale.*

Finally, scrunch up your toes (as if you've stepped in something gooey). Keep holding the tension and then release after ten seconds. Observe the relaxed feeling in your feet and toes.

Now that you have relaxed your muscles from head to toe, take a couple of minutes to focus on breathing slowly and deeply. As you breathe, imagine yourself becoming even more and more relaxed. When you're ready, slowly draw your attention back to your surroundings. Open your eyes, and carry this feeling of relaxation with you as you continue your day.

Section Six

Conclusion

26 maintaining your progress

Danielle was diagnosed with generalized anxiety disorder (GAD) when she was fourteen years old, after her parents took her to see a cognitive behavioral therapist to make changes in the way she dealt with her worries. Over the course of six months, she and her therapist used many of the activities in this workbook to better understand the types of unhelpful thoughts getting in her way and to gradually let go of behaviors that were actually making her anxiety worse. Given her tendency to believe her friends were mad at her and her classmates were criticizing her (mind reading), she found it most helpful to find evidence for and against these beliefs (challenging worry thoughts, hypothesis testing) and to gradually stop trying so hard to make everyone happy (people pleasing). She also found that spending less time on social media and more time getting sleep were key to reducing stress about social situations. By the time she finished this workbook, her therapist pointed out that her next step was to make sure she continued to use her skills whenever worry showed up again. Danielle learned to notice her personal signs that indicate worry is becoming more of a problem for her—for instance, if she has trouble sleeping for more than a few nights in a row, catches herself reading too much into her friends' facial expressions (*Are they mad?*), or goes overboard to please others even if it takes time from other things she has to do. Danielle knows that when these signs show up, it helps her to review the workbook sections that were most helpful to her and use the worksheets that will get her back on track.

Like Danielle, after making your way through this workbook, you've acquired comprehensive skills and strategies for reducing the role that worry plays in your life. Specifically, you have learned to

- map out your worry cycle of thoughts, emotions, physical feelings, and behaviors;

- understand different types of distorted "junk mail thinking";

- manage worry thoughts by acknowledging and ignoring them, distancing yourself from them, challenging them, or just sitting with them;

- stay in the present moment through mindfulness techniques;

- gradually expose yourself to feared situations and test out your worried predictions;

- understand, identify, and eliminate safety behaviors (that is, time-consuming and unhelpful actions that masquerade as "protective");

- use problem solving to your advantage;

- tackle common stressors effectively;

- create beneficial exercise and sleep habits; and

- use progressive muscle relaxation proactively to reduce stress.

You have been working hard! Hopefully, you're noticing how this hard work has made your worry less intense and disruptive so that you can devote more time and attention to the people and activities you care about most.

As you have mastered these strategies and skills, it's important to keep up the good work by continuing to incorporate them into your life whenever worry shows up. For Danielle, that meant noticing when her old worry habits became a problem again, like getting stuck on thoughts that her friends were upset with her and spending a lot of time pleasing others. These thoughts and behaviors were a signal to her that it was time to go back and review the strategies and skills that worked for her in the past.

for you to do

Regular practice of your skills will lead to sustainable improvements in worry over time. Take a moment to identify the activities that have been most beneficial in helping you break your worry cycle. Review the Contents, or flip through the workbook as a refresher, and write down your own personal top five activities and their corresponding page numbers for easy reference:

1. _____ Pages: _____

2. _____ Pages: _____

3. _____ Pages: _____

4. _____ Pages: _____

5. _____ Pages: _____

Going forward, notice signals that your worry cycle is ramping up again. It's not uncommon for junk mail thinking and safety behaviors to show up again during times of stress, like a major transition (for example, starting high school or going to college), a change in your family or friendships (for example, an argument with your best friend, your parents deciding to separate), or having too many activities on your plate. But even in the absence of stress, you might notice signs that worry is causing you some trouble, like when worry thoughts and behaviors

- take up more time out of your day;

- get in the way of participating in activities or enjoying time with family or friends;

- increase in intensity (or bother you more);

- are more challenging to ignore;

- lead to difficulty sleeping or concentrating; or

- cause physical discomfort (like muscle tension or headaches).

In addition, think about your own personal signs of worry—specifically, the types of junk mail thinking, safety behaviors, and other forms of avoidance that have previously given you trouble. Write these personal warning signs below. As a guide, Danielle wrote this:

I know my worry cycle is starting up when I

1. *Have trouble sleeping for more than a night or two.*

2. *Get stuck on mind-reading thoughts.*

3. *Catch myself spending too much time looking for signs that my friends are upset with me.*

4. *Go overboard trying to make my friends happy.*

Now, it's your turn.

I know my worry cycle is starting up when I:

1. _____

2. _____

3. _____

4. _____

Whether you're in the midst of a stressful time and want to proactively manage any worry that shows up, or you notice some of the above signs that the worry cycle is starting up again, you can take action to maintain the improvements you have made throughout this workbook. Revisit the top five activities you wrote down at the beginning of the exercise. Read the activities in detail and use the worksheets provided for a few weeks to a few months (that is, until the time of stress has passed, or until worry has become less intense and disruptive again). Feel free to photocopy the relevant workbook pages or visit http://www.newharbinger.com/35845 to download forms and complete additional helpful activities and exercises.

You have done some impressive work! Though I know it hasn't always been easy, I want to congratulate you on taking such good care of yourself—you have put in the time, energy, and consistent practice to make excellent use of the skills presented in this workbook. Congratulations on investing and believing in yourself while gaining valuable tools that will help you confidently manage your worries now and for a lifetime to come!

acknowledgments

I am grateful to all of the fantastic mentors and colleagues I have had in my career for teaching me how to understand and effectively treat people with anxiety disorders—in particular, my mentors in graduate school at Boston University (Jill Ehrenreich-May, Donna Pincus, Sara Mattis, and David Barlow), my many dedicated supervisors during training at Massachusetts General Hospital (MGH), and my mentors (Dina Hirshfeld-Becker and Aude Henin) and colleagues in the Child CBT Program at MGH.

I have been so fortunate to have the love and support of my friends and my family, including my parents (Jerry Micco and Patricia Schraff), my sister (Laura Micco) and brother-in-law (Colin Redman), my mother-in-law (Jean O'Hara), my father-in-law (Wayne O'Hara), my daughters (Violet and Layla), and especially my husband, Scott O'Hara, who gave me the time to complete this project and lots of encouragement along the way.

Finally, I am endlessly appreciative of the many worried teens I've evaluated and treated over the years—I've learned the most through my work with such a brave and impressive group of young people.

references

American Psychiatric Association. 2013. *Diagnostic and Statistical Manual of Mental Disorders: DSM-5.* Washington, DC: American Psychiatric Association.

Asmundson, G. J., M. G. Fetzner, L. B. DeBoer, M. B. Powers, M. W. Ottow, and J. A. Smits. 2013. "Let's Get Physical: A Contemporary Review of the Anxiolytic Effects of Exercise for Anxiety and Its Disorders." *Depression and Anxiety* 30: 362–73.

Biegel, G. M., K. W. Brown, S. L. Shapiro, and C. M. Schubert. 2009. "Mindfulness-Based Stress Reduction for the Treatment of Adolescent Psychiatric Outpatients: A Randomized Clinical Trial." *Journal of Consulting and Clinical Psychology* 77: 855–66.

Burstein, M., K. Beesdo-Baum, J. P. He, and K. R. Merikangas. 2014. "Threshold and Subthreshold Generalized Anxiety Disorder Among US Adolescents: Prevalence, Sociodemographic, and Clinical Characteristics." *Psychological Medicine* 44: 2351–62.

Cajochen, C., S. Frey, D. Anders, J. Späti, M., Bues, A., Pross, R. Mager, A. Wirz-Justice, and O. Stefani. 2011. "Evening Exposure to a Light-Emitting Diodes (LED)–Backlit Computer Screen Affects Circadian Physiology and Cognitive Performance." *Journal of Applied Physiology* 110: 1432–38.

Hayes, S. C., K. D. Strosahl, and K. G. Wilson. 1999. *Acceptance and Commitment Therapy: An Experiential Approach to Behavior Change.* New York: Guilford Press.

National Sleep Foundation Sleep and Teens Task Force. 2000. *Adolescent Sleep Needs and Patterns: Research Report and Resource Guide.* Washington, DC: National Sleep Foundation. Available at http://www.sleepfoundation.org/sites/default/files/sleep_and_teens_report1.pdf.

Otto, M. W., and J. A. J. Smits. 2011. *Exercise for Mood and Anxiety: Proven Strategies for Overcoming Depression and Enhancing Well-Being.* New York: Oxford University Press.

Jamie A. Micco, PhD, is a licensed psychologist in private practice in Concord, MA, and a lecturer in psychology at Harvard Medical School. She received her PhD in clinical psychology from Boston University, completing her clinical and research training at the Center for Anxiety and Related Disorders. Thereafter, she was a staff psychologist at Massachusetts General Hospital, where she most recently served as the director of an intensive cognitive behavioral therapy (CBT) program for youth with severe anxiety. Micco specializes in CBT for children, adolescents, and adults with anxiety disorders, obsessive-compulsive disorder (OCD), and depression.

More ⏱ Instant Help Books for Teens

An Imprint of New Harbinger Publications

**OVERCOMING
PROCRASTINATION
FOR TEENS**

A CBT Guide for
College-Bound Students

ISBN: 978-1626254572 / US $16.95

**THE ANXIETY WORKBOOK
FOR TEENS**

Activities to Help You Deal
with Anxiety & Worry

ISBN: 978-1572246034 / US $14.95

**THE ANXIETY SURVIVAL
GUIDE FOR TEENS**

CBT Skills to Overcome
Fear, Worry & Panic

ISBN: 978-1626252431 / US $16.95

STUFF THAT SUCKS

A Teen's Guide to Accepting What
You Can't Change & Committing
to What You Can

ISBN: 978-1626258655 / US $12.95

THE MINDFUL TEEN

Powerfull Skills to Help You
Handle Stress
One Moment at a Time

ISBN: 978-1626250802 / US $16.95

**THE PERFECTIONISM
WORKBOOK FOR TEENS**

Activities to Help You Reduce
Anxiety & Get Things Done

ISBN: 978-1626254541 / US $16.95

newharbingerpublications
1-800-748-6273 / newharbinger.com

(VISA, MC, AMEX / prices subject to change without notice)

Follow Us 🅵 🅣 🅸 🅟

Don't miss out on new books in the subjects that interest you.
Sign up for our **Book Alerts** at **newharbinger.com/bookalerts**

Register your **new harbinger** titles for additional benefits!

When you register your **new harbinger** title—purchased in any format, from any source—you get access to benefits like the following:

- Downloadable accessories like printable worksheets and extra content

- Instructional videos and audio files

- Information about updates, corrections, and new editions

Not every title has accessories, but we're adding new material all the time.

Access free accessories in 3 easy steps:

1. Sign in at NewHarbinger.com (or **register** to create an account).

2. Click on **register a book**. Search for your title and click the **register** button when it appears.

3. Click on the **book cover or title** to go to its details page. Click on **accessories** to view and access files.

That's all there is to it!

If you need help, visit:

NewHarbinger.com/accessories

new harbinger
CELEBRATING
40 YEARS